D1200890

ALSO BY SIEGFRIED ENGELMANN:

GIVE YOUR CHILD A SUPERIOR MIND
  (*with Theresa Engelmann*)

TEACHING DISADVANTAGED CHILDREN IN THE PRESCHOOL
  (*with Carl Bereiter*)

CONCEPTUAL LEARNING

PREVENTING FAILURE IN THE PRIMARY GRADES

TEACHING: A BASIC COURSE IN APPLIED PSYCHOLOGY
  (*with W. C. Becker and D. R. Thomas*)

Your Child Can Succeed

How to Get the Most Out of School
for Your Child

Siegfried Engelmann

SIMON AND SCHUSTER   NEW YORK

The author wishes to thank Allyn and Bacon for permission to quote from Education for the Open Society *by Aubrey Haan, copyright © 1962, Allyn and Bacon, Inc., Boston; and William C. Brown Company for permission to quote from* Corrective Reading *by Miles V. Zintz, copyright © 1972 Miles V. Zintz.*

DESIGNED BY ELIZABETH WOLL
MANUFACTURED IN THE UNITED STATES OF AMERICA
BY THE BOOK PRESS, BRATTLEBORO, VT.

1   2   3   4   5   6   7   8   9   10

LIBRARY OF CONGRESS CATALOGING IN PUBLICATION DATA

ENGELMANN, SIEGFRIED.
   YOUR CHILD CAN SUCCEED.

   INCLUDES BIBLIOGRAPHICAL REFERENCES.
   1. READING (ELEMENTARY)   2. ABILITY GROUPING IN
EDUCATION.   I. TITLE.
LB1573.E69   372.1′1′02   74–22416
ISBN 0–671–21944–8

Contents

Preface

Of the many books written about the schools and their problems, many call for reform. The authors of most of these books use what seem to be plausible, even compelling, arguments about our commitment and love for children and the flagrant practices that occur in many schools. Based on the authors' analysis of the problem, a solution follows. This book follows the same format. There is, I hope, one difference. This book attempts to deal with the real issues. While the authors of many of the other books may have strong social feelings and possess the ability to write persuasive prose, they seem to lack knowledge about the most critical problem in the schools today—the lack of regard for instruction. The typical solution that is offered in these books is to change the format of instruction, change the teachers' attitudes about minority children, or engage in some near-magic solution that has little relationship to the specific inadequacies in the schools that result in the problem.

The theme of this book is that children can be taught if we employ the technology needed to teach them. Similarly, children can be motivated if we stop leaving the motivation to chance and engineer the behavioral changes we desire in kids. The underpinning of this theme is that we have a strong moral and economic commitment to our children, and this commitment must be manifested with more than love. It must be translated into successful action.

The book discusses typical abuses. These are not presented in a highly "documented" way because these abuses are so common that a visit to the nearest elementary or junior high school will probably verify them. Rather, the book attempts to provide a typical portrait of failure, the kind experienced by both the disadvantaged child and the middle-class child. Even though there are many differences in the makeup and backgrounds of these children, they share two important characteristics—they have the capacity to succeed in academic subjects, and their failure experiences are remarkably similar. An objective of the book is to show it the way it is, without reference to the most flagrant or atypical abuses.

I have worked with many school districts, and I have taught all kinds of kids, from autistic to high-school dropouts, from deaf to orthopedically handicapped. Furthermore, I have seen that it is possible—but not necessarily easy—to achieve highly impressive results with all of these children if careful instructional procedures are followed. I have also seen that teachers are more often quite willing to learn successful techniques and quite capable of mastering them. Although this book frequently attacks teachers, please understand that I have a high regard for them and I am sympathetic with their problems. They, like the failure children, are products of their education, and like the children they too can be changed.

Although I feel qualified to write this book, my views may be prejudiced by personal or economic investment. I am the author or co-author of various instructional programs. To the best of my ability, however, I have not let my personal investment in these programs influence the arguments I present in the book. I have tried to follow the abiding formula that kids come first and other interests must not conflict. The schools, the teachers, and instructional programs have a single purpose: to provide children with the kind of education that will allow them to make the broadest range of choices about their adult life. The more children have been taught in school and the wider the variety of skills they possess, the greater the number of options that are available to them.

I am sure that the arguments in this book will be strongly contested by different educators. However, I feel that the case that I present is valid, and the evidence is contained in most schools. My case may not convince you, but I hope that it makes you curious enough to investigate what is going on in your schools. The observations you make may both surprise and horrify you.

SIEGFRIED ENGELMANN

1

The Stage and the Cast

Today was a staffing day, and, as on other staffing days, Mary was restless. She felt that the restlessness was prompted by uncertainty about her adequacy. Had she actually provided the best possible instruction for those third-grade boys who were to be "staffed"—Jimmy and Andrew? Had she read the signs correctly? Had she done all that was possible to achieve the delicate balance that results in learning? These questions, she realized, would probably never be answered. As she drove to the school that morning, she kept reminding herself that she had tried. Still, there was that echo of reproof. Had she tried *everything?*

She pulled into her parking place near the office and went into the school. The secretary said, "Good morning, Miss Gibbs. Mrs. Walker is waiting to see you." The secretary nodded in the direction of the principal's office.

Mrs. Walker was Jimmy's mother. She didn't seem to understand that there were individual differences among children, just as with anything else in nature. She seemed to have the eminently unenlightened view that children could be taught to read by the clock, regardless of how mature they were, what degree of readiness they had achieved, or what type of emotional makeup they had.

Mary went into the office, where the principal, Mr. Morris, was seated behind his desk. Mr. Morris said, "Sit down, Miss Gibbs. We were just talking about Jimmy."

Mary forced a smile for Mrs. Walker and said, "Well, as I believe I told you the other day, Mrs. Walker, we are having a staffing today. And we're going to try to work out a course of action for Jimmy."

Mrs. Walker said, "Are you going to put him in a special class? I know very well that Jimmy is not retarded. He's a smart boy—and a good one. If he's not reading, maybe it's not entirely his fault."

"Perhaps you're right," Mary said patiently. "There are many factors that determine whether or not a child is ready to read."

Mary was half tempted to tell Mrs. Walker that one of the factors was parental acceptance and that another was the degree of cooperation between the parent and the school. How much of Jimmy's problem had been caused by a mother who couldn't accept Jimmy as an individual, as a boy who had not been endowed with the same nervous system, the same interests and motivation as the "average" child? It seemed obvious to Mary that Mrs. Walker represented the epitome of parental blindness. Parents should not force children into a single mold; they should recognize that a child is a living, breathing individual. And Jimmy was creative in art; his use of language was excellent, often precocious; and his insight into social situations sometimes surprised Mary. There was the time that Jimmy had witnessed a fight between two older boys, one of whom was a bully. In recounting the incident, Jimmy had said, "I think everybody wants to feel important. Some guys even have to be bullies to feel important."

Mr. Morris said, "I assure you, Mrs. Walker, that Jimmy will receive the most highly professional consideration that one could find anywhere in the state. As Miss Gibbs has probably told you, we are fortunate enough to have an excellent staff and the resources needed to help children like Jimmy."

Mrs. Walker bristled. "What do you mean, 'children like

Jimmy'? Is Jimmy a freak? From the beginning, I've had the feeling that the plan is to convince me there's something wrong with Jimmy. And there *isn't*."

As patiently as possible, Mary told her, "We went through all of this the other day. I tried to explain to you then that Jimmy is not performing at third-grade level in reading. He is quite a bit below. I don't think it would be advisable to show you the achievement tests that have been given to him, but I can assure you that Jimmy has a problem."

"What are you going to do with him? Hold him back a year?"

Mr. Morris said, "There's been no decision yet. That's the purpose of the staffing meeting this morning. Dr. Stein, Dr. Gliessen, Mrs. Anderson, our social worker, Miss Gibbs, and I are meeting in a few minutes. We hope to arrive at a plan for Jimmy. And believe me, Mrs. Walker, the idea is to work out a plan that is best *for Jimmy*."

"But . . ." Mrs. Walker said. Her voice trailed off and her chin quivered. "I just don't know where we went wrong. We tried to be good parents. We had lots of books around the house. My husband plays with Jimmy a lot. They build things. They're building a model train now. It's a freight train with all kinds of cars, and a bridge and . . . I just don't know."

Suddenly, Mary felt sorry for Mrs. Walker. She put her hand on Mrs. Walker's shoulder.

"It's not your fault," Mary said. "Children read when they are ready. But they're not all ready at the same time. You wouldn't expect them all to develop at the same rate any more than you would expect all of the lilies in a garden to bloom at the same moment. Nobody is to blame. And you certainly shouldn't blame yourself. Accept Jimmy for what he is. Don't blame him or yourself for what he is not."

How many times had Mary said this to parents? The words came out as easily as the names of letters in the alphabet.

Mrs. Walker wiped her eyes. She said, "I guess you're right. I don't know who or what to blame. But isn't there something we can do? Can we get a special tutor for Jimmy? Is there some place we can send him for treatment?"

"You're perfectly free to," Mary said. "But Jimmy works hard in school. When he goes home, he should do things that other eight-year-olds do. He shouldn't come home tired and have to work on reading. I don't feel that the extra work will pay off. The best thing that you can do for Jimmy is to see to it that he has good attitudes toward school and that he is well rested and well fed. Let him know that you love him and that you don't feel that he has failed you by not learning to read. We will do the rest for Jimmy."

Mrs. Walker stood up. She nodded to Mr. Morris and to Mary. In a hoarse voice she said, "Thank you." She walked to the door. Mr. Morris followed her. She said, "You will let me know what you decide?"

Mr. Morris smiled. "I'll call you this afternoon."

As Mary stood there in Mr. Morris' office, she wasn't sure whether she had given Mrs. Walker too much hope for Jimmy. Mary had almost implied that Jimmy would read. But would he? The chances, Mary figured, were about fifty-fifty that Jimmy would be a disabled reader. Mary had seen many Jimmys. Some of them had gone through a sudden spurt of growth and learned to read. Others hadn't, despite Mary's best efforts.

Mr. Morris was back. "What kid wouldn't have problems with a mother like that?" he said. "And she comes on as if she's got all the answers. I was half tempted to tell her to take the kid out of school if she didn't like the way we were handling him."

"I don't know," Mary said. "I wouldn't want my child to fail in reading. I can appreciate the way she feels."

"Oh, I can, too," Mr. Morris said. "I'm always glad when parents come in. Gives us a chance to engage in some meaningful dialogue and share our ideas. The part that gets me is that some parents come in with a bad attitude. They're not asking. They're telling."

Mary nodded. She didn't like Mr. Morris. There was something sneaky and dishonest about him. Most of the other teachers seemed to feel the same way.

"Well," he said, patting himself on the abdomen, "we've got about five minutes before the meeting."

Mary said, "I'll see you there. I want to go to Room 120 for a moment."

She walked down the corridor, noting to herself that it was a very pleasant school. The large picture windows, the ceramic tile, the audio-visual center—all blended together to form a learning environment far different from the one Mary had experienced as a child. Mary had gone to school near the steel mills. There were no reading coordinators or learning centers in her school. There were blackboards that were black and teachers who were old. Mary had to admit, however, that she had liked her grade school. For a moment Mary experienced a fleeting memory of sitting at a desk reading—escaping.

Mary was standing in front of Room 120. She rapped on the window and waved to the classroom teacher, Mrs. Bronson.

Mrs. Bronson opened the door. "Hi," she said. "Do you want to see Andrew?"

"Yes," Mary said. "I can't work with him for the full period, but I would like to review a couple of things with him."

When Mary entered the room, some of the children whispered, "Hello, Miss Gibbs." Mary responded with waves and smiles. She stopped at the desk of Andrew, an unfortunate black boy who had never received the learning opportunities most children take for granted. Mary had worked with Andrew since he had been in the first grade. He was a third-grader now, but he was a disabled reader—a failure. "Come on, Andy," she said. "Let's go over what we learned yesterday."

Mary took Andrew to her room, the reading room, designed for working with one child or a small group of children. It was well outfitted with everything from a tachistoscope to a variety of reading and perceptual-motor equipment. Andrew went directly to the balance board.

"No," Mary said. "We're not going to do that today. We're going to go over sounding out words." Mary believed strongly that children must learn basic motor skills before they can learn to read. She routinely had them work on the balance board and engage in other types of hand–eye coordination exercises (as well as those designed to enhance the child's perceptual ability). Andrew was very good at the motor games. He was quite agile on the balance board and superior in the other motor games. Despite his performance in these activities, however, he couldn't read.

Mary wrote the word *mat* on the green chalkboard. "Do you remember this word, Andrew?" She tried not to show that she was anxious. She wanted to say, "Please remember it. Please, damnit."

Andrew studied the word. Then he smiled. "*Can,*" he said.

"No, it's not *can,*" she said. "Can you figure out what it is?"

"Wan me soun i ow?" he asked.

"Yes, Andy. That's how we figure out words that we can't recognize."

Andrew touched the first letter. "Mmmm," he said, looking at Mary. She nodded. He moved to the next letter. "Aaaa," he said. Nod. Last letter: "Tuh." Nod.

"Do it again, a little faster." Mary couldn't control the edge of irritation in her voice. *Please figure it out.*

"Mmm . . . aaah . . . tu. . . . Mmmmm . . . aaaah . . . tu."

"What word?" Mary said quietly.

"Mu-ahtu."

"Tell me the word, Andy."

"I dunno."

"Let's try it again. I'll say the sounds with you this time."

Mary directed Andrew's finger quickly across the letters. "Mmm, aaa, t," she said. She repeated the sounding-out two more times. Then she said, "What word?"

"*At?*" Andrew said, searching her face.

"No," Mary said quietly. "It's not *at.*"

"*Cow?*" Andrew said.

"Oh, Andy," Mary said. "How can that word be *cow*? You know better than that. The last letters form the word *at*. That's one of our basic words, isn't it?"

"Yeh?" Andrew said.

"*At*. And then we put the *mmm* in front of the *at* and what word do we have?"

"I dunno."

"Of course you do. The first letter is *mmm* and the rest of the word is *at*."

Andrew's stare seemed to get cold. He turned toward the word on the board and looked at it. After a moment, Mary said, "The word is *mat*."

"Mat," Andrew said blankly.

Mary had hoped to cover more ground, but the time had gone by already.

She said, "I'll see you tomorrow, Andy. You can go back to Mrs. Bronson now."

Andrew left. Mary fixed her hair, took the files on Andrew and Jimmy from her desk, and went to the conference room.

Mrs. Anderson and Dr. Stein, an optometrist, were seated at the table. Mr. Morris was standing in front of the window. Mary greeted the others and sat down. Just as she opened her files, Dr. Gliessen, the school psychologist, came in.

"Hi, gang," he said. Then to Mary, "Have you thought over that idea I had about you and me teaching sex education with a practicum experience?" He winked, and Mary could feel herself start to blush. Everybody laughed.

Mr. Morris said, "That sex education stuff is no joke anymore. I had a parent call this morning complaining about the biology that we're teaching in the sixth grade. She as much as said that it was part of a Commie conspiracy."

The others started to talk about sex education. Mary turned back to her files. She looked over the familiar graphs and figures. She saw nothing new and half wondered why she was studying the test results.

Dr. Gliessen said, "Let's get started."

The first child to be discussed was Jimmy Walker. Dr. Stein gave his report on the child's visual capacity. The child's performance was good on the vision test: twenty-twenty. Jimmy was not color blind. "However," Dr. Stein said, "it seemed apparent that the child had an emotional reaction to color. Jimmy was fascinated with the yellow spots on the test cards. I'm no psychiatrist, but I understand that this kind of behavior may be symptomatic of early forms of psychosis."

Dr. Gliessen said, "Well, it may be. It's true that schizophrenics are sometimes hooked on the color yellow."

Dr. Stein nodded. "Yes," he said. "Another observation that I made during the testing was the child's apparent restlessness and poor attention span."

"Was he uncooperative?" Mrs. Anderson asked.

"Not exactly. In fact, he seemed to be going out of his way to be cooperative. But I got the idea that his behavior was forced, as if he was trying abnormally hard to succeed."

"Yes, yes," Mrs. Anderson said. "I have some interesting things along that line."

"Okay," Dr. Stein said. "We might as well move on to you. I don't think the boy has ambliopia, although he has definite preference to use his right eye, which is not abnormal. His visual discrimination seems adequate. I don't think we'll find a problem there. I think the problem has more to do with how he uses the visual information that he receives from his eyes."

Mr. Morris nodded and gestured toward Mrs. Anderson.

She said, "Jimmy's health record shows that his mother had a very difficult pregnancy with Jimmy. She had a history of miscarriages and she had to avoid physical exertion throughout her pregnancy with Jimmy. Labor was induced. Jimmy had a very high fever when he was two years old. They suspected encephalitis, which could well account for his brain damage. The picture that I get from interviews with the parents is that they are overprotective. The father spends a great deal of time with the boy, and I don't really think that Jimmy has an opportunity for the peer encounters he should have. The mother is latently hostile toward the close affective ties between father and son. I believe that she feels quite ambivalent about the relationship. On the one hand, she has a strong, sometimes neurotic, need for Jimmy to succeed. On the other, she is in competition with the boy over the father's affection. As a result, she vacillates between pushing the child and wanting to see him fail."

Mrs. Anderson turned toward Dr. Stein. "This is the part that I feel relates to what you observed in the testing situation. Jimmy is a very sensitive boy. He wants to please his mother. She makes him feel guilty about not succeeding in school. With all of this pressure on him, he naturally tries very hard to succeed in every situation. He wants people to appreciate him and to want him. Every situation is symbolic of his relationship with his mother. He is trying to compensate for the lack of her approval."

Mr. Morris nodded. "I can see that. The boy's got emotional problems."

"That's putting it mildly," Mrs. Anderson said. "I talked to his mother about going to a therapist so that she could learn to understand her own motives better, and you should have seen her reaction. Rather than face the issues, she started to attack *me* and *my* motives. It was quite plain that I had struck a very tender nerve."

Dr. Gliessen asked, "Do the parents fight and argue in front of the child?"

"I can only surmise what goes on in the house," Mrs. Anderson said. "But the father has alluded to the fact that he does not lead an entirely happy life. He indicated that he hates his job. He's an advertising executive. And one of his big joys is playing with the boy. It is also quite possible that he has a drinking problem. I went out to lunch with him and he had two double martinis."

"What's wrong with that?" Dr. Stein said. "I think he's got the right idea."

Everybody laughed. "Seriously," Mrs. Anderson went on, "I see both parents as living through the boy, or at least as using the boy as a pawn to satisfy their own neurotic needs."

Everybody was quiet for a moment. Then Mr. Morris said, "Well, I think it would be safe to say that the boy has emotional problems."

Dr. Gliessen said, "I don't think that what I have will add that much to the discussion. I gave Jimmy seven tests." Dr. Gliessen thumbed through his file and pulled out some papers. "He has a very strange profile on the Illinois Test of Psycholinguistic Ability. He was very high in most of the categories, but he was low in motor encoding and visual memory."

"I'm sorry," Mrs. Anderson said, "I'm not familiar with the test. What do the results mean?"

"Well," Dr. Gliessen answered, "I'm not sure." He looked at the ceiling and blinked several times. "Typically mentally retarded children score poorly on visual memory. But the Walker boy is not retarded. His IQ on the Stanford-Binet is 127, which is pretty good."

"Could emotional factors account for his performance?" Mrs. Anderson asked.

"Well . . . I guess so. Something is strange."

Mr. Morris said, "Why don't you give us a quick summary of the boy's performance on the various tests—if that wouldn't take too long."

"All right," Dr. Gliessen said. "I've already told you about the Illinois Test and IQ. On our version of the MMPI [Minnesota Multiphasic Personality Inventory] the boy showed very poor self-image. He feels that he will fail in situations where others will succeed. And he doesn't have very high expectations for himself. But he's not paranoid. He feels that other people like him."

Mrs. Anderson said, "Is it possible that he can't accept the fact that others don't like him, namely his parents, and that he therefore pretends that people like him—as a kind of denial that he has been rejected?"

Again Dr. Gliessen stared at the ceiling. "Well, I guess so.

The trouble is, you don't get any clear tendency from the test. Maybe that's the clue." He blinked. "He tends to be normal but there are strange little aberrations in his performance. For example, on the figure-copying test, his performance was very immature—like that of a five-year-old." Dr. Gliessen brought some drawings from his folder, passed them around, and continued. "I think I noticed the same tendency that has already been referred to. Like when he was making these drawings, he would look up from time to time, as if he wanted me to tell him that he was doing all right. He'd do the same thing after answering IQ questions. He seemed very anxious for me to tell him that he was doing all right. Of course, I couldn't tell him. I had to follow the test procedures."

Mr. Morris said, "Would it be safe to say that Jimmy is immature and emotionally disturbed?"

"I don't know," Dr. Gliessen said. "He's probably got affective problems of some sort, but I don't think we can call him emotionally disturbed."

Mrs. Anderson said, "I think we would be on professionally safer grounds if we said that he had emotional problems—these overlaid on immaturity."

Dr. Gliessen said, "There's one more thing. Tests of neurological maturation and other visual-perception skills show that the boy is dyslexic, which means that he is fundamentally incapable of reading. He does not have the neurological integration necessary for the complex skill of reading."

"Miss Gibbs, do you have anything to add?" Mr. Morris asked.

"No, not really," Mary said. "I have the records of two years of frustrations. We tried various reading methods. When it became apparent that Jimmy was doing a great deal of word guessing in the Wonderful World series, I first tried some additional work with phonics. We also worked on the Frostig perceptual-motor program. And, of course, we did a series of small and large motor exercises. The results were anything but encouraging, so I tried some other things, including several programs that have recorded some success with retarded children. But it's always the same. One day he'll remember the rule about the two vowels that walk together, and the next day he'll use the rule on a word that doesn't have two vowels. He tries, but . . ."

Everyone was silent. Then Mr. Morris said, "Okay, let me see if I can summarize. We have a boy with emotional problems who is immature in some respects, although he performs well on some tests of mental ability. And he's dyslexic."

Mary felt a little relieved with the pronouncement that Jimmy was dyslexic. It meant that Jimmy would probably never read according to adult standards, but at least Mary wasn't at fault.

"Now comes the big question," Mr. Morris said. "What do we do with him? He's finishing the third grade. Where does he go from here?"

Mrs. Anderson replied, "It seems to me that he's had enough pushing to last him some time. I think that he should be put in a program that is suited to his level of ability. It would be a hideous form of punishment to put him in a regular classroom where he'll only become increasingly frustrated and ultimately hostile."

"I don't know that I agree with that," Dr. Gliessen said. "I think the boy has to be treated as a specific learning disability. We can't put a lad with an IQ of 127 in a special class—no way. I think we should leave him in the regular classroom and take him out every day for reading instruction. We won't expect miracles from the instruction. But we can't put him in a special class."

Mrs. Anderson said, "That's what I meant when I said that we shouldn't keep him in a regular class. I wasn't implying that we would put him in a class for the retarded." She laughed and shook her head.

Mary said, "I'll go along with Dr. Gliessen's suggestion. I can work with him on perception games and some of the exercises that he can do easily. Maybe he'll gain a feeling of success."

Dr. Stein said, "This is getting a little out of my ball park, but won't Jimmy be in trouble if he's the only one in the class who can't read? What's he going to do when the other children are working on history or science if he can't read the book?"

Mary said, "We have a multilevel system. It's not like the typical 'grades' that they still have in some schools. The reason is that in an average fourth grade children vary in reading ability all the way from the first to the eighth grade. It's ridiculous to assume that they should all work from the same book on the same material. We organize projects in science and history in which the children learn things and make reports. The readers who are not so mature are given assignments that don't tax their ability."

"How well does this plan work?" Dr. Stein said.

"Fine," Dr. Gliessen said. "No problem—well, at least not more than a few hundred a day."

There were a few chuckles around the table. Mary managed a smile. Dr. Gliessen said, "Is that it on Jimmy? Anybody got anything more to say?"

Mary looked at the faces of her staffing colleagues. They looked back at her.

Mr. Morris said, "Okay, Dr. Stein, what do you have on Andy?"

"He probably should have glasses. His vision seems all right, but he squints a lot, especially when he's working up close. It may be that some of his problems result from a sensitivity to light. In any case, it wouldn't do any harm to fit him with a pair of tinted glasses."

Mrs. Anderson said, "I think we can do that with our state assistance funds for the educationally disadvantaged." She patted her folder. "This is very interesting—the home situation. I tried for a week to get hold of his mother. No luck. So I finally went over there. It's quite a neighborhood. The Merelin house is almost beyond description. Dilapidated, crawling with kids of all shapes and sizes. And the smell!

"When I knocked, Angela, Andy's ten-year-old sister, answered the door. I asked her why she wasn't in school, and she gave me a sheepish smile. I asked if her mother was home and she said, 'Na.' "

Mrs. Anderson shook her head. "The family moved here from Chicago last summer. The mother works all day. The father is probably in the Navy. Nobody knows for sure. The grandmother and an aunt live with the mother. There are either eleven or twelve children in the family. Andy's Head Start record shows that he was beaten almost to death when he was three. That may have been the cause of his brain damage. The social worker in Chicago indicated that Andy wouldn't use the toilet in the Head Start classroom. She investigated the problem and discovered that he had been traumatized several years before by finding a rat in the toilet at home. This experience probably evoked a series of fantasies about feces. In the kind of environment in which Andy lives we can well imagine the kinds of fantasies that were evoked.

"One more thing. I think that Andy's grandmother is senile. She gave me an incredible lecture on how the spirits control everything. And she is the one who takes care of Andy when he's at home."

"It's a wonder that any kid ever makes it in that kind of environment," Mr. Morris said.

After a few seconds of silence, Dr. Gliessen said, "The testing that I did shows that the boy is clearly retarded. Whether this retardation is due to lack of learning opportunities or whether it is organic I can't say. His IQ is seventy-four, placing him in the range of educably mentally handicapped. His language development is about that of a five-year-old, and less than that on language analogies. His memory, strangely enough, is very good. He was above age level on a test in which he was asked to repeat random digits. This fact would tend to indicate that he is culturally and not organically retarded."

Mrs. Anderson said, "I can't agree. Isn't it true that some organics have memories for very specific things but not for others?"

"Yes," said Dr. Gliessen. "Some schizophrenics who are retarded in everything else sometimes exhibit strange memory skills, such as being able to multiply four-digit numbers by four-digit numbers in their heads."

"That's what I thought," Mrs. Anderson said. "I keep thinking of the beating that Andy had when he was three. I would guess that in addition to any impairment resulting from lack of educational opportunities, the boy is suffering from brain damage. There's something about the way that boy looks and about his posture that just isn't right."

Dr. Stein said, "You may be right. He had trouble with the test of peripheral vision. It may be that his visual field is somewhat impaired, which could be associated with brain damage."

Dr. Gliessen said, "It's possible. I think we could safely say that he has MBD—minimal brain dysfunction. Developmental data would support this. I'm just a little hesitant to say for sure that he has brain damage. I can't really see a clear picture of this from his performance on the tests."

Mr. Morris said, "For the record, can we agree that we can safely say that he has MBD?"

Mary said, "I don't think he's brain-damaged. He's so good on the motor exercises. He has good balance, good hand–eye coordination."

Dr. Gliessen said, "Mary's got a good point. His good motor skills are a sign of good neurological integration. He doesn't exhibit any postural or space-orientation problems that you typically find in children who have verified histories of brain damage; but he has short attention span and he tends to be hyperactive. I think he's MBD."

Mrs. Anderson smiled. "I still have a gut feeling that the boy is brain-damaged."

"Maybe we'd better play it safe and say simply that he's retarded. We don't have to indicate the cause," Mr. Morris replied.

Mary nodded. So did Dr. Stein and Dr. Gliessen.

Mr. Morris said, "Now comes the big question. What do we do with him?"

"You don't have any choice," Dr. Gliessen said. "He's got to go into a special class."

Mr. Morris drummed on the table. "I hate to do that. Do you realize that in our pre-primary special class over half of the kids are black? We're busing in only something like forty-five kids, and over a third of them are in special classes. It's going to look as if we're operating segregated classrooms if we put any more black kids in those classes."

"What else can you do?" Dr. Gliessen said. "Andy won't have a prayer of making it in a regular class."

Mary said, "His achievement tests are pretty bad. He scores below the beginning first-grade norms in almost everything."

"Isn't there something else we can do?" Mr. Morris asked. "Isn't there some way we can keep him in the regular classroom?"

Mrs. Anderson said, "Why put the child in a situation he can't cope with? How can he be expected to relate to the teachers and his peers if he is made to feel alienated from them by the academic work? I think he'd be much better off in a situation that was tailored to his abilities. You can't give him that situation in the regular classroom."

"That's right," Mary said. "I desperately wanted Andy to succeed. I've spent a great deal of extra time with him. I remember a professor of mine once told me that a teacher is ill advised to spend additional time trying to bring low children up to grade level. I thought he was inhumane. Now I think I understand what he was trying to tell us. All I succeeded in doing with Andy was probably to frustrate him and make him feel like a failure." Mary recounted the session with Andy before the staffing. She concluded, "What Andy needs is work suited to his ability. He's got to succeed on simple material. What he doesn't need is more pushing to keep him in the regular class."

Mr. Morris held up his hand. "Okay. I'm convinced. Although I hate to do this, Andy goes to the special class."

Everybody nodded.

Mary felt good as she picked up her file and started toward the door. Now that she could work with Andy in a pressure-free situation, one in which no grade-level goals were expected, she would have a greater chance to share with him. Mary had long been an admirer of Sylvia Ashton Warner, and Mary believed that in the special class she would be able to follow the Ashton formula: to find words that had a deep emotional significance to Andy and, working from these, to simultaneously build a reading vocabulary, an understanding vocabulary, and a communication bridge between Mary's world and Andy's.

Professionals or Frauds?

The scene with Mary and the others takes place in most school districts. Perhaps the procedure is not as formal in some districts; perhaps not as many people are involved. The trial, however, is basically the same. That's what it actually is, a trial, the outcome of which is predetermined. The child is guilty. The only problem facing the judges who take part in the staffing is to state the child's problem in such a way that the problem is clearly his. He must be the one responsible for his failure. This point must be made clear so that the school, the administration, and the teachers are fully exonerated.

This is not to say that the people involved are vicious. Like most of us, they merely reflect what they have been taught. And they may possess all of the ancillary credentials of the professional—the concern, the vocabulary, the apparent objectivity. What they lack is an understanding of what teaching is all about. Dr. Stein, for example, would like to believe that vision and visual perception occupy a position of preeminence in reading and all other subjects. He would be quite pleased if it were true that "ambliopia" and other visual problems advertised on TV cause reading failure. Unfortunately, there is no evidence to support his claim. And there is a great deal of evidence to support the conclusion that if the child has enough vision to find his way into the classroom, he can be taught to read, assuming the reading instruction is actually that—careful instruction in reading.

Dr. Gliessen would like to believe that his tests and his analyses of them tell something about the child, perhaps probing beyond mere phenomena and tapping the springs of ability and mental processes. He sees the intelligence test as a test of innate capacity. He doesn't see it as an achievement test that samples from the various skills children may be taught. He sometimes has trouble reconciling the fact that the intelligence test is supposed to measure the child's capacity with the fact that there are Andys in the world, disadvantaged children who are as retarded as any child in the special class—children who cannot be changed by taking them on a trip to a zoo or exposing them to "culture" and a variety of "stimulating experiences." Dr. Gliessen's best rationalization is that the lack of learning opportunities in the ghetto situation seems to depress the capacity to learn, in much the same way that not watering a young plant may result in stunting. Dr. Gliessen uses tests. Yet the driving purpose the tests serve is to provide a rigorous procedure for labeling a child with such names as "dyslexic," "developmentally immature," or "anxious," words that are expressly designed to tell both the teacher and the parents, "It is not our fault that the child failed. He is dyslexic. *HE is at fault—not you, not I.*"

The idea never really occurred to Dr. Gliessen that Jimmy is disabled because he was never *taught*. Dr. Gliessen is not only ignorant of the technology of instruction; he doesn't really believe that there is such a thing. He believes that the development of children is inevitable within limits. He believes that one can depress a child's performance but that there is no way to increase the performance of a retarded child. There is no way to teach a dyslexic child, he believes, unless one first discovers some way of reorganizing the central nervous processes that are currently inhibiting the normal development of the child. The unfortunate aspect of this formula is that the teacher never observes the child's central nervous system. She deals only in behavior.

Mrs. Anderson considers herself a first-rate liberal. She believes that the schools should respect individual children and see to it that each child is psychologically adjusted. She would like to see the schools adopt a combination of the British infant school (which allows children to choose whether or not they will learn) and Summerhill. She would like to see young boys and girls naked in school, interacting without frustration and pressure, each encouraged to become a unique, well-adjusted person. Mrs. Anderson recognizes that her beliefs are a little too advanced for her school district. She doesn't recognize that her Freudian model is a trap. If one wishes to hold the position that Jimmy's mother is a neurotic, one can find the evidence to support this conclusion. If one wishes to argue that she is not neurotic, one can use the same evidence. Freudian arguments are good insulation. Mrs. Anderson's contention that Jimmy's mother's reactions indicate a basic neurosis insulates Mrs. Anderson from even considering the possibility that Jimmy's mother may be accurate in her description of Jimmy and her appraisal of the problem. If Jimmy's mother had been agreeable, Mrs. Anderson probably would have argued that the mother appeared to be too indulgent. If Jimmy's mother had been nervous, Mrs. Anderson could have made a case for latent guilt. So long as Jimmy's mother breathed, Mrs. Anderson could have constructed a case against her. She simply had to wait for the behavior that was remotely consistent with Mrs. Anderson's gut feelings.

Mr. Morris too knows nothing about instruction. He doesn't see that he has any part in instruction, so long as there are no serious disruptions in the classroom. He tells people that he has a marvelous staff and that there is no reason for him to concern himself with the nuts and bolts of the classroom. He doesn't know if his teachers are good. He likes order, and so long as his teachers maintain order (or so long as the parents don't complain about apparent disorder) he is satisfied. He has no role to play in monitoring each teacher's performance. He does not demand a performance standard from them. He knows the names of some of the basal series that are used in different classrooms, but he is not familiar with the minute-by-minute operations of each teacher. Each teacher is an island, an unquestioned, unmonitored, unaccountable entity. Mr. Morris wouldn't consider assuming the role of an advocate for the children and telling a teacher precisely what he expected her to achieve with various children. Granted, there have been times when Mr. Morris had to step into the classroom and restore order. There have also been times when Mr. Morris knew that teachers were not performing, but he was not quick to correct these situations, because he didn't want any trouble with teachers' unions or with the higher administrators in the district (the first people to hear about it if he were to become "too tough" with a teacher). The children obviously suffered, but Mr. Morris didn't concern himself with them. He simply reassured himself that his school was as good as any in the district; and his teachers were probably better than most. The fact that an occasional classroom of children gets wiped out is unfortunate but inevitable.

It is interesting that neither Dr. Stein, Dr. Gliessen, Mrs. Anderson, nor Mr. Morris understands instruction. None was taught procedures and techniques needed to bring about desired learning. None is clearly aware that there is a technology of instruction or that it can be as precise and powerful as surgical techniques. Even more interesting is the fact that the last member of the group, Mary, was trained in elementary education, even received a master's degree in reading instruction, has worked with children for six years, and knows no more about instruction than the others. We will return to Mary later.

2
What Is Teaching?

Does "Teaching" Change the Child's Behavior?

If you were to ask your superintendent of schools or your local teacher organization the simple question "What is teaching?" you would hear many words. You would perhaps be told that there is a difference between teaching and "training." You would learn that teaching is a process, not a mere product, and that the teacher is responsible for the process. You would discover that teaching is an interaction of some sort, in which child, material, environment, and teacher participate. The outcome is contingent upon the relative mixture of these ingredients. If you were persistent and kept asking the question "What is teaching?" it would become apparent that your question was not being answered. You would realize that your respondent did not describe teaching so that you would be able to discriminate between teaching and a host of other activities. He certainly teased many of the peripheral aspects of teaching and seemed to assume that you already know what teaching is. But he did not come out and say what it is.

Here is the issue: Mary spent time with Andy. She devoted a great amount of time to him. She cared. But did she actually teach? There are two possible answers. One is that she went through teaching motions, therefore she taught. The other answer is that Mary hasn't taught until the child demonstrates that he is capable of doing the things she tried to teach.

During the past five years, the question "What is teaching?" has been posed with increased frequency to many school districts and many colleges of education. In the overwhelming number of cases no answer was received. Teacher union regulations were cited; state laws and certification requirements were quoted; but the question remained unanswered. Has a teacher taught reading after she goes through the assigned pages in the textbook, following the statutory procedures, or has she taught reading only after the children in the classroom demonstrate that they are now able to read? No answer. Would a teacher be teaching if she went through the program at twice the prescribed rate, four times the rate, perhaps forty times the prescribed rate? No answer. If a teacher teaches, what does an aide in the classroom do when the teacher turns a child over to her and says, "Work on beginning letter sounds with Tommy"? No answer.

Several recent issues in the schools have brought the question of what teaching is into focus. The first is performance contracting, or contract learning. Contract learning assumes the position that teaching happens only when the children can demonstrate that they have been taught. The contract that the school system makes with some outside agency is to improve the performance of the children in a subject, such as reading. The contract may indicate that for every child improved one full year in reading performance, the contractor will receive so much money. The contractor is not paid for any child who does not show the one-year gain in reading ability. Those children who do not perform have not been taught the minimum skills scheduled for a year's "teaching."

The most general reaction of teachers' unions and traditional school administrations to performance contracting is negative, and perhaps for good reason. The schools have been designated as the agency responsible for teaching the children. Why should the schools contract with another agency to do the school's job? On the other hand, performance contracting is a commendable concept based on the assumption that the children can be taught and that they are taught only when they can demonstrate skills that they couldn't demonstrate before instruction. Performance contracting takes a very solid stand on the question of what teaching is.

The other issue that has brought attention to the question of what teaching is relates to the status of aides in the classroom. According to the traditional view, aides are supposed to reinforce, augment, and supplement the teacher's instruction. The teacher is supposed to "introduce" new material to the children. The aide takes it from there. In practice, the traditional guidelines aren't always clear in the daily classroom routines. Is the aide *teaching* when she works with a child or a small group? Did the teacher *teach* when she "introduced" the new material or concept?

In 1969 I had my first opportunity to present the question "What is teaching?" to an official body that could give an answer. The place was a rural Midwestern community with a federally sponsored program for poor kids. Our group (the University of Oregon Follow Through model) was working with the community. In the classrooms that participated in the program, both the teachers and the aides *taught;* that is, they performed in highly similar ways when working with children. While the classroom teacher worked with one small group in arithmetic, one aide worked with another small group in reading and a third aide worked with a group in language. The aides had been chosen primarily from the parents' group.

The local school authorities became quite critical of the program during its second year and tried several ways of dumping it. First they challenged the program's effectiveness, indicating that the children were not performing well. At the time, the children who completed the first grade scored on the middle-third-grade level (as measured by the Wide Range Achievement Test). After several other abortive ploys, the administration seized upon the teacher-versus-aide issue.

I was called to meet with members of the local school district, the teachers' association, the parents' group, CAP (Community Action Programs), the State Department of Public Instruction, the Office of Economic Opportunity, and the Office of Education. My objective at the meeting was this:

I wanted the state to make a statement about what teaching is. If the statement held that teaching did not have anything to do with the performance of the children, but was limited to the teacher's motions or behaviors, the state would be hard pressed to explain why only a certified teacher can deliver the teaching monologue.

If the state maintained that the teaching had nothing to do with the performance of the teacher or the performance of the children, the state would admit that there is no such thing as teaching and that there is no point in having teachers or schools, because there is no way of showing that the teachers are doing that thing called teaching.

If the Department of Public Instruction admitted that teaching is related to the performance of the children, the state would be faced with such questions as (1) Do all teachers successfully change the performance of children? and (2) Are some aides capable of doing a better job than some teachers?

The answers to these questions could be determined by looking at the performance of the children, since the performance would constitute the only admissible evidence about whether teaching had taken place. If investigation disclosed that some aides actually teach better than some teachers, the state would be in the very awkward position of trying to reconcile state certification requirements with the facts about "teaching." The state would be guilty of certifying nonteachers and at the same time denying certification to people who could actually *teach*.

The meeting, held in an elementary-school classroom, was far more interesting than I had anticipated. It was packed with officials and legal counsel. A representative of the State Department of Public Instruction got things going by reading a statement that squelched most of the attack I had planned. The essence of the statement was that the state would not specify which jobs or responsibilities were those of teachers and which were those of aides. The state would not articulate what teaching was in performance terms, insisting, rather, that the question of teacher and aide responsibilities is a *local concern.* The state had no objections to the aides "teaching" in the program, so long as such teaching was acceptable to local school authorities.

A representative of the teachers' union, who saw the movement of aides teaching as a plot to remove all teachers and replace them with lower-salaried aides, read a statement from the State Department of Public Instruction that spelled out the business of teachers providing the initial teaching while aides reinforce, complement, and supplement instruction. After reading the statement he said, "This is the official position of the state, so we have to take it as the last word."

The state department representative stood up and said, "I wrote that letter, and I'm telling you that it is not the last word. Ignore it. The last word is the statement that I read earlier." He then reiterated points in the latest statement.

The superintendent said, "It still bothers me, the idea of aides teaching. We all know that teachers are trained. Aides are not. Teachers go to college a long time. They have skills that you can't expect an aide to have."

The first respondent was the legal counsel for the regional CAP. "Bullshit," he said. "There is no legal assumption that a teacher has skills. She has a certain *legal* responsibility, as defined by state law. And that's it."

Then the state representative said, "So far as this state is concerned, there is no assumption that a teacher has any more skills than the man on the street. There is nothing either in training or in certification procedures that would assure any kind of exceptional skill. What the teacher does have is a responsibility— not a skill, merely responsibility. She is in charge of the classroom. She is responsible for the children's safety. The state, however, makes no assumption of exceptional skill."

During the morning coffee break, I told the state representative that I really appreciated the stand he was taking.

He smiled and shook his head. "I know your game," he said. "You want me to say that teaching has something to do with the performance of the children. You want me to say that the teacher is *supposed* to have skills that aides don't have. I'm not going to make any such statements. Do you realize what would happen in this state if we specified what teaching is in terms of specific performance? We have over three hundred experimental programs that would be wiped out tomorrow. We have Title One programs in which older children tutor younger children. Are the older children teaching? We have programs in which people from the community conduct seminars. Are these resource people teaching or reinforcing? Can you imagine what would happen if we described teaching in terms of performance? What about programmed material? Is *it* a teacher? And what about computer-assisted instruction? We might discover that we have to give our computers sick leave and vacations. No, thanks."

Many of the more harmful practices of the school result from the simple fact that *the "system" has not clearly decided whether there is such a thing as teaching.* The federal government is trying to effect a change by providing funds to programs that show results. In several states, school projects that are to receive additional state and federal funds must include some kind of performance criterion. For the typical school system, however, these innovations have made only the most modest impact. These systems have not yet considered the question "What is teaching?"

The Burden of Proof Is with the Child

Like many teachers, Mary doesn't know what teaching is. If we were to ask her, "Do you teach?" she would indicate that she does. She could produce children who can read and who weren't able to read before she started working with them. If we were to ask her about some of the other children, such as Jimmy and Andy, Mary would indicate that some of them are immature, some are just not ready, some lack motivation, some are emotionally disturbed, some brain-damaged, and some just plain slow. Mary's position is plausible on the surface. When we examine it more critically, we see that Mary is using a floating standard. If she manages to teach a child, she takes credit for the teaching: "I taught him to read." If he fails after instruction, however, Mary does not say, "I did not teach him to read; *I* failed." Instead she implies that the child is at fault: "*He* did not learn, because of some fault that *he* has." Under these rules, whatever the system wishes to call "teaching" automatically becomes teaching, and those children who do not respond to such teaching are garnished with labels.

By using a floating standard, Mary insulates herself from the problem, avoiding responsibility for her failures. She "hopes," but doesn't feel obliged to find a technique that works, because in the back of her mind she *knows* that the child is at fault. She never has to say, "I didn't teach Jimmy. I'd better take a good look at what I did, so that I don't make the same mistake again. I'd better find out why *I* failed." Rather, she can feel satisfied that she provided the child with all the teaching that he "should" require.

The schools often use subtle means of underscoring the theme that the child is to blame for failure. One is to place a strong emphasis on that which is visible and physical, following the simple principle of making the physical surroundings look as if learning must be taking place. The idea is to convince any sensible person who makes a casual observation of the school that any child failing to learn in such surroundings must have something wrong with him.

The learning center (or library) in the school is supposed to convey the idea that children are doing a lot of independent reading and learning even if such learning is not happening. The experimental equipment in the classroom is designed to convince the rational observer that the children are conducting exciting experiments and are learning from these experiments. Even lavishly illustrated textbooks are supposed to convey the impression that these would "motivate" children to read them. The school is designed so that it *appears* conducive to learning.

The schools, however, do not usually assume direct responsibility for the performance of the children. Rather, they see their role as "providing an opportunity for the children to learn." Some children take advantage of these opportunities; others don't. If a child doesn't choose to learn from a given experience, *the child is blamed*. The schools take the child's failure to learn as *evidence* that there is something wrong with the child. They argue that other children have learned successfully from the same experiences; therefore, there must be something abnormal about the child who doesn't choose to learn from a given experience.

Was Andy Taught?

The school's attitudes about teaching and learning can be illustrated by referring to a specific child, Andy, who had been exposed to a rather typical program. His first exposure occurred in 1967, when he was four years old. The federal government's poverty program was in full swing, and Head Start was being billed as the primary vehicle that would do away with the second-class citizen. Head Start literature, written in the style of the Madison Avenue slick, promised great IQ gains for the "culturally deprived" by acquainting them with culture—a trip to the zoo, a mirror so that they could see themselves, toys, even a language program. Actually, Head Start was an expensive front for public health. The "educational component" of Head Start had been turned over from the medical men to a group of noneducators who usually operate from the department of home economics at universities—the early-childhood educators. Their model of teaching young children is the typical nursery school, their objective to nurture children in the same way that a cornstalk is nurtured: provide food, water, and fertilizer; then let nature take its course. Translated into specific techniques for Andy, this meant a Head Start classroom that was open so that the children "would not feel restricted." There were many toys. The dress-up corner would "build the child's self-image, by helping him learn who he is." The sand table and the easels would give Andy a chance to "be creative, express himself, and discover that his creative efforts are accepted by the teacher." The teacher, of course, was to work from the children's interests, starting with those concrete experiences that are "meaningful" to the children.

The stage is set for the children to come into the classroom. At first they are quiet, but soon they start to test the limits. Trucks fly through the air. Children are crying. Well-intentioned teachers are chasing children, yelling at them. After three months, the children have "settled down" to a point where the three adults in the classroom can sometimes manage the fifteen children. During part of the day (when the children are not taking off their wraps, going to the bathroom, putting on their wraps for recess, taking off their wraps after recess, having their snack, eating lunch, and putting on their wraps to go home) the teachers manage to engage some of the children in "learning activity." There is no specific program.

Let's sit in on one of these "learning activities."

"Look at what I have," the teacher says, holding up a card that illustrates a red ball. The teacher then points to various cards on the floor in front of six four-year-olds. "Who can find a card that is the same color as this card?"

The little boy next to Andy holds up a card with a yellow ball on it. A little girl picks up three cards and puts one of them into her mouth.

Andy looks at the teacher for a moment before returning his attention to his shoelaces.

"Listen, boys and girls. I want you to find a card that is the same color as the card that I have here."

Two of the children hold up the cards that they have selected. A girl shows two cards. None is identical to the teacher's.

Apparently unperturbed, the teacher picks up a card with a picture of a red apple. "This card is the same color as the other card that I have. Andy, look at the cards. Andy . . ."

Andy looks tentatively at the teacher. He doesn't look at the cards. Instead, he looks intently at her face, trying to figure out her game.

"Andy," she continues, "look at the two cards. They are the same color, aren't they?"

Without removing his stare from her face, Andy nods yes.

The teacher says, "And what color are the ball and the apple?"

"Re . . ." a little girl shouts.

"Re . . ." two other children mimic.

The teacher says, "They are red, aren't they, Andy?"

Andy nods yes.

"Can you find something else that is red?" the teacher asks.

Andy looks at his shoes. He then points cautiously in the direction of three or four cards.

"Is one of those red?" the teacher asks.

Andy nods and says, "Yeh," almost inaudibly.

The teacher picks up a card that displays another red apple. "This is red, isn't it?" she says. "Were you pointing to this card?"

Andy glances quickly at the card and then back to the teacher's face. He nods yes.

"Leon," the teacher says, "what color is this?"

"Re . . ." Leon says loudly with his hands over his ears.

The teacher then holds up a card showing a green evergreen tree. "And what color is this?"

"Re . . ." Leon says.

"Re . . ." one of the little girls says.

"Re . . ." Andy says.

Did the teacher actually teach anything through this activity? Six of the fifteen children in the room did not learn the names of even three colors by the end of the year, although the teacher spent twelve hours of "learning activities" similar to the one we observed. If we judge teaching in terms of the outcomes or the performance of the children, the teacher certainly did not teach.

Andy's Head Start teacher would probably use the "readiness" argument to explain the performance of the children. According to this argument, a teacher "exposes" children to different concepts or experiences. Those children who are "ready to learn" learn from these exposures. Those who are not ready must wait until they become ready. This argument is pervasive in traditional education, but very dangerous. It does not call for any accountability on the part of the teacher except perhaps to expose the children to "concrete examples," and to tell the truth. Andy's teacher certainly satisfied these requirements. Her presentation wasn't very successful in changing the children's behavior, however.

Can the Demonstration Teach?

We can go a step further and ask, "Was it *possible* for her presentation to teach *all* of the children?" This question may not seem fair. We know that children differ in their ability to learn. For the moment, however, let's not look at the children. Let's look at the concept that the teacher tried to teach and see if her presentation was capable of teaching it to a very intelligent being who didn't happen to know what *red* meant.

Since red is the same for all people, it is reasonable to begin with a simple analysis of the concept to see what it is that all people must learn about red. Red is a visual property. It is not dependent on the size of the object or on the object's position, shape, or texture. The first requirement of a demonstration designed to teach red, therefore, would be that the demonstration make it clear that red has only to do with that visual property of redness. Andy's teacher did not satisfy this requirement. All of the red objects were round, implying that red may have something to do with shape. Therefore, we could expect that a being with superior intelligence might come away from the teaching demonstration confused about the meaning of red. Specifically, this being might show us through his behavior that he thinks that *red* is another word for *round object,* or that red is something that applies only to two-dimensional objects on a card.

Since the presentation would not be consistently capable of teaching a naïve being with superior intelligence, maybe Andy, Leon, and some of the other children are not completely at fault for not learning from the demonstration. Maybe they would have responded well to a demonstration that carefully showed what *red* means. We can't make any clean assertions about the problems the children might have had, but it seems presumptuous to declare that the children were not ready or that they should have been able to extract the appropriate interpretation from the teacher's presentation even if it was not logically possible to do so.

It is sometimes difficult to explain the difference between a demonstration that will teach and one that won't. Because adults are familiar with concepts such as red, they have trouble recognizing that these concepts are not picked up automatically.

For this reason, let's refer to a made-up concept. Let's say that a teacher presented each of these objects:

The teacher says that each is a "glerm."

Next, the teacher presents this object and asks you if it is a glerm:

The response of virtually any child or adult would be "Yes."

Now the teacher presents this object and asks if it is a glerm:

We cannot predict what your response will be. If we present the task to thirty different people, we can predict that over half of them will say, "Yes, it's a glerm." The others will say, "No, it is not a glerm."

In any case, some who respond will fail the task. The response of those who fail, however, is a *reasonable response*. Both responses are consistent with the presentation of the objects. One person might interpret the presentation this way: "The teacher showed a group of objects. All were rectangles and all were called glerms. Then the teacher presented another rectangle and asked if it was a glerm. I said, 'Yes.'"

Another person might interpret the presentation this way: "All of the initial objects were vertical. It seemed more than accidental that all were vertical. The teacher then presented a rectangle that was not vertical and asked if it was a glerm. I said, 'No.'"

While the "glerm" example may seem far removed from the classroom situation, the "glerm" format is perfectly analogous to the one that the naïve child encounters in the classroom. The teacher says a strange or unfamiliar word. She then gives an example that illustrates the word. She may say the word *red* and present an object that is an example of red, perhaps a picture of a red apple. "See? It's red," she says. And from this kind of demonstration the child is supposed to figure out what *red* means, just as you had to figure out what *glerm* means. The child must try to figure out whether the word *red* means an apple, something shiny, something the teacher is holding, the color of the object, or the position, or whether it is simply a word that the teacher uses arbitrarily.

Since any of these interpretations is consistent with the teacher's presentation, we shouldn't conclude that the child is "slow" for selecting a wrong interpretation. The labeling should be deferred until the teacher has provided a presentation that is far less ambiguous.

Learning Concepts from an Object

In some early-childhood programs, such as Andy's Head Start program, teachers were encouraged to use a single object as the point of departure for teaching about many concepts. On one occasion, Andy's teacher used a Teddy bear as an example of softness, furriness, brownness, something with two ears, eyes, legs, and a tongue. Andy didn't understand what *two* meant. He wasn't sure what *ears* meant. He certainly didn't understand the meaning of the words *brown, soft, furry,* and *tongue.* These words were like noise to him. To Andy, the teacher's presentation must have sounded something like this: "See, it's emememe. And notice it's rmemem. It has tutut rmemem, doesn't it? And . . ."

The teacher assumes that her demonstration with the concrete object will make these words meaningful to the child. The assumption is somewhat incredible if we consider that *an object is never an example of a single concept.* A shoelace is not merely an example of "shoelace." It is also an example of a color, of a cloth object, of an object with ends, and so forth. If we were to add up the concepts that adhere in common objects, we would find that most have at least twenty. For the teacher this means that it is impossible to show what a concept means by presenting a single example, yet teachers consistently assume that single-object presentations will teach. These teachers have been encouraged to believe that the child views the world in a way quite different from the adult view. The child's logic is seen as such a mysterious development that teachers are encouraged not to ask such questions as "Is it *possible* for anybody to learn from the demonstration that I have provided?"

The traditional view which deals almost exclusively with the child and the way he learns displaces the problem. We have to look at the concept we wish to teach to see whether the demonstration is capable of teaching. The children's responses will give us some feedback, but we will never design adequate teaching demonstrations if we look only at the children.

Most teachers who work with young children espouse some form of the child-logic philosophy and therefore often ask children to do the impossible. They suppose that children can learn from single-example presentations, apparently never becoming aware of the contradiction.

From what we've said about real teaching so far, it is possible for us to state two important principles. The first is that it is never possible for a teacher to teach basic concepts by presenting only a single example of the concept. The second is that the teaching demonstration must admit to only one interpretation. To achieve a real teaching demonstration, the teacher must show what the concept is and what it isn't.

The necessity of "not" examples was illustrated by Andy's Head Start teacher. Near the end of the year, she decided to teach the children the names of the letters. On three or four occasions, she presented the letter *b*. She had the children color in *b*'s. Later, when she introduced *d,* she was surprised to discover that even her best "students" called the letter *b*. The teacher discussed the problem later with some of her colleagues. They agreed that the Head Start children have severe visual-perception problems. Actually, visual perception had nothing to do with the children's performance. Their mistake was as reasonable as indicating that a vertical rectangle is a glerm. Consider that a chair is a chair whether it is upside down or right side up. In fact, every object the typical four-year-old has encountered has the same name regardless of the object's position. Then a teacher presents b and d and expects the children to know that each has a different name *even though* b *is the same object as* d. It is merely in a different position. Ironically, the teachers typically conclude that the *children* have perceptual problems.

To ensure that all children have an honest opportunity to learn *b* and *d,* the original teaching demonstration would have to show the children what "not-b" is. Here is such a demonstration: The teacher presents a transparency on which b appears. When the transparency is flipped over, the b becomes a d. The teacher presents the b side of the transparency. "This is the letter bee," she says. "What is it?"

"Bee."

Now she turns the transparency upside down. "Is this bee? *No.*" She turns the transparency ninety degrees. "Is this bee? *No.*"

Back to b position. "Is this bee? Yes."

She flips the transparency over. "Is this bee? . . ."

She repeats the demonstration until all of the children are able to respond correctly to her questions. She then repeats the demonstration with a different b, a bigger one in a different color. This demonstration further shows the children what b is and what it is not. When the two parts of the demonstration are coupled, the children are left with one interpretation: "When the object b is in a particular 'position' it is called 'b.' When it is not in that position it is not referred to as 'b.' " Later, the teacher can show the children that one of the "not-b" positions is called d, another is called p and another is called q.

Andy never received such a demonstration. By the time he completed the third grade, *five* years after his school instruction began, his understanding of b was glazed and hazy. He supposed that there was some kind of mystery associated with b and d. If he could express his confusion, he might say, "That funny object is sometimes called d by the teacher, sometimes b, and sometimes something else. The teacher probably calls it different names when she feels like it, or when it appears in words that have particular significance."

The b/d problem is not trivial. We have been working with groups of junior-high-school kids who have reading problems. Not a single child in one of these groups could read the following clause without making a b/d mistake: ". . . but the big bug dug until the bell went ding." The irony is that these children could have been easily taught b and d in preschool, kindergarten, or the first grade. Although the "corrective work" we have provided has resulted in substantial improvement in reading accuracy, it would have been far more humane to prevent the problem through teaching demonstrations that admit to a single interpretation.

Demonstrations with Misrules

A few years ago, several investigators conducted an interesting experiment relating to the basic principle that demonstrations consistent with more than one possible interpretation cause some children to mislearn. Their "hypothesis" was that if a child produces appropriate responses when presented an object, learning will take place. The experiment was rather clever. Nonreading middle-class children were presented color words such as *red, green, blue, black.* Each word was written in its color. The children, all of whom knew colors, quickly learned to identify or "read" the words. They were producing the correct responses in the presence of each stimulus. On subsequent days, the color of each word was "faded." Now the word *red* was not solid red but red interspersed with black dots. Each day the colors were faded further, until there were merely a few specks of red on the word *red* and a few specks of yellow on the word *yellow.* The children were still responding correctly to each word. Then the final step: the last of the color was removed from each word. To the surprise of the investigators, and contrary to their hypothesis, the children did not produce the "responses" they had been producing before. Most of the children now called every word "black."

The reason was basic: the presentation of these words was consistent with more than one interpretation. To respond correctly during the initial presentations, a child could attend either to the configuration of the word, to its color, or to both. Either way, he would get the right answer. Since the presentation admitted to more than one possible interpretation, some of the children keyed on the color. The rule that they selected was,

"Identify the object by referring to the nonblack color of the object. If it has no nonblack color [like the word *black*], identify it as black."

Actually, it is possible to predict whether a teaching presentation will lead to confusion. In the experiment above, we could predict that some children will select the wrong interpretation. We can also predict that if the teacher teaches a group of naïve children to count to three (the most common number selected by teachers), some children will learn a serious misrule. Here is generally how the misrule is implied: The teacher demonstrates. "Watch me count to three: one, two, three." She often talks about what she has demonstrated. "I counted to three." Then she usually has the children practice the counting with her. "Let's count to three: one . . . two . . . three."

After ten to fifty exposures, the children will be firm on counting to three. But now the teacher presents a new task, such as counting to five. Before she can even demonstrate the counting, however, she will probably discover that the children have learned a misrule. "Now we're going to count to five," she says.

And some of the children respond, "One . . . two . . . five."

Clearly, differences in the examples that the teacher presents *cause* differences in the way children learn and respond. This phenomenon can be demonstrated with nearly any group of naïve children. Although the children who give the wrong response rarely receive credit for their ingenuity, they are pretty smart kids. They picked up an interpretation that is perfectly consistent with what the teacher showed them.

The Rules a Child Learns

The examples of glerm, red, reading color words, and counting to three illustrate a much discussed educational phenomenon, generalization—that children differ in their ability to generalize. Though this is quite true, what the traditional interpretation doesn't consider is what generalizes when a child responds to an example he has never seen before. Let's say that he indicates that a new object is "red." Something transferred, but it was nothing concrete. The only thing that could have transferred is an abstract rule about what you must observe in an object before you declare that it is red. Similarly, a child who says, "The cat is under the chair," although he has never seen that cat under that particular chair before, is showing us through his behavior that he has formulated a precise rule about the kind of relationship that is referred to as "under." (He also shows that he understands the rules for expressing this relationship.) What transferred cannot be explained in terms of "association" or anything less than an abstract rule.

Chomsky and other linguists have pointed out that children learn abstract rules about grammar, citing the behavior of the children as evidence. Since the children generate sentences they have never heard before, they must have "learned" something that would account for such performance. The only thing that could account for the performance is a specific and often complicated rule.

We can extend Chomsky's argument to a host of situations that don't involve "grammar." In fact, by using the same basic argument—which is that we must specify some learning that could account for the child's performance—we must conclude that there are very few learning situations in which the children are not required to formulate abstract rules that are quite complicated.

And these rules are perfectly consistent with the examples to which the child has been exposed. In other words, a presentation is consistent with interpretations or abstract rules. The child formulates a rule and applies it to new examples. If the presentation is clean, the appropriate rule will be applied. Presentations consistent with more than one interpretation cause some children to formulate the wrong rule.

If this explanation of generalization seems incredible, try to figure out what transfers when a child calls an object he has never seen before a "shoe" or calls the mailman a "daddy." It's either magic or an abstract rule. If it's magic, we don't need teachers.

A Definition of Teaching

At the beginning of this chapter, we posed the question "What is teaching?" We are now in a position to define, or at least describe, teaching. We noted that the teacher's presentation actually causes the children to respond in different ways. We have seen that if the teacher presents only a single example of a concept, some children will not learn. If the teacher presents a poorly constructed set of examples, some children will pick up a misinterpretation. If the teacher does not show the children what the concept is *not*, some children will generalize beyond the scope of the concept (calling *d* "bee"). In every case, what the teacher does *causes* a difference in what the children are taught. That's the central notion of teaching. The teacher must cause the children to learn. A teacher hasn't taught when she says a prescribed number of words or presents so many examples. She has taught only when the children can demonstrate that they have learned the concept. The teacher must take responsibility for the children's performance. She must use examples, tasks, and her technical skill to bring about the appropriate performance. She must also be prohibited from blaming the children for not learning when she has provided a demonstration that is incapable of teaching.

Here is a consistent definition of teaching: *Teaching is the manipulation of environmental variables to cause predicted behavioral changes in the children.*

Consider the first part of the definition: the manipulation of environmental variables. This part tells us that the teacher cannot use drugs or surgical instruments to produce the changes in the children. She must work from the "outside," using the things that are available in the environment. She can present examples; she can praise or scold; she can give instructions, ask questions, point to things, and correct. She can talk loudly, whisper, yell, laugh, or cry. She has no direct access to the child's brain, his inner self, his capacity to learn. If she is to affect these, she must do so by manipulating environmental variables.

Consider the last part of the definition: teaching causes predicted behavioral changes in the children. This part says simply that the proof of teaching is the behavioral changes that take place. A teacher hasn't taught reading until a child can read. The activity that is designed to teach reading may or may not teach. If the activity causes the desired outcome in a particular child, that activity taught the child. If not, the activity was a flop. Note that the behavioral changes in the child must be predicted. Some have suggested that work on a balance beam results in teaching behavior. The fact that the balance-board activity causes changes in the child's behavior does not mean that the activity is reasonable. The activity must fulfill the prediction of enabling children to read before it can be accepted as a reasonable prereading activity.

There is more to teaching than the examples the teacher presents. The way the teacher acts when she is teaching causes the children to respond in specific ways. If the teacher moves slowly, the children will lose interest in what she is doing. If she uses many words the children don't understand, she will cause some of the children to "turn off" and not listen to what she says. If she doesn't show the children through her behavior that what she is presenting is exciting and important, she will cause some of the children to treat the material in a very indifferent manner. If she doesn't correct the mistakes that the children make, she will cause some of the children to become confused—even though her presentation of examples is adequate. In every case, a difference in the way the teacher behaves causes differences in the way the children respond and how they learn. That's what teaching is—causing predicted changes in the child's behavior.

It is understandable why schools often shy away from the simple conclusions about what teaching is. The description of teaching we have provided clearly places responsibility on the teacher, not on the children. The description implies a different type of teacher training—and monitoring system—than one finds in most schools. It implies different methods of testing and diagnosing children. Also, it implies a moratorium on the kind of labeling that goes on in schools. Most of all, it implies a change in focus. The central concern of the schools should be to protect the children, not to misteach them and then blame them for their failure.

3

The "Theory" Behind Labeling Children

Jimmy Walker entered kindergarten with an IQ of 120. He devoured readiness material during his kindergarten year. He failed in school. His failure didn't begin in the third grade or the seventh but in the most critical grade, the first. He failed to master the most important steps in reading—the first steps.

The reading series used in Jimmy's school is a sight-word-reading program, sometimes referred to as look-and-guess. The philosophy on which sight reading is based is that the children learn to read whole words, rather than learning about the letters that compose words. Jimmy's first-grade teacher was an advocate of the sight-reading approach. That was the approach endorsed by the college she attended.

Jimmy was in the top reading group at the beginning of his first-grade year. Each day, when the teacher announced that the A group was to read, Jimmy felt excited. The teacher instructed the children to open their readers to the appropriate page. Each page showed an illustration of the characters, Bill and Sally, involved in some activity. Beneath the picture was a sentence or two that told about the picture. The teacher said, "Everybody, point to the words as I read them." She then read, "Bill and Sally went to the lake." Next she called on different children to "read" the sentence. According to the teacher's guide that accompanied the program, the teacher was to help children who made errors by asking them, "What word would fit in that sentence?" If necessary, she encouraged them to look at the picture to find additional "cues."

During the first part of the year, she rarely had to correct Jimmy. He could "read" any of the sentences the teacher had gone over in class. When she called on him, he glanced quickly at the picture, pointed to each of those things called words and read, "Bill . . . and . . . Sally . . . went . . . to . . . the . . . lake." Jimmy paused between the words because it seemed the thing to do. He could actually "read" much faster if he wanted to.

Around November things changed. The teacher called on Jimmy to read a new sentence, one that the teacher had not first introduced. Jimmy looked at a picture that showed Bill and Sally washing their dog, Buff. Jimmy pointed to the words and read in his most fashionable manner, "Bill . . . and . . . Sally . . . washed . . . their . . . dog."

"Oh, Jimmy," the teacher said. "I'm surprised at you. Try it again. This time, look at the words more carefully."

Jimmy repeated his original narration, this time somewhat more uncertainly, glancing up at the teacher from time to time. The teacher shook her head. "No, Jimmy," she said. What was wrong? Jimmy had told about the action illustrated in the picture. His narration sounded as good as any of the others he had memorized.

The teacher pointed to the fourth word in the sentence. "That word isn't *washed*. It's a word we've had. You should remember it."

Yes, Jimmy said to himself. The teacher had mentioned something about looking at "the beginning of the word." But which part was the beginning?

"That word begins with *g*," the teacher said.

"*Garden*," Jimmy said.

Two girls in the group giggled. A couple of boys followed

with chortles. The teacher said, "Now, Jimmy, would that make any sense, to say that Bill and Sally 'garden'?"

Jimmy looked at the word as intently as he knew how. He felt his ears burning. He wanted to cry, but he didn't. He tried to pierce the word with his eyes. He squinted. He opened his eyes as wide as they would go. Finally, and a little timidly, he said, *"Get?"*

All of the children in the group laughed. "Lorraine," the teacher said, "tell Jimmy that word."

"Gave!" Lorraine announced.

"Yes," the teacher said. "Lorraine, you may read the entire sentence."

" 'Bill and Sally gave Buff a bath.' " Lorraine glanced at Jimmy and smiled. Jimmy wanted to run home. But he sat there and looked at the sentence. He tried to burn the page into his mind. He looked at the picture and then back to the sentence. He pointed to the words and said them to himself several times.

How Much Is Jimmy Worth?

Jimmy's mother had cried on the first day of kindergarten, watching her nearly grown-up son, overdressed and oversupplied, as he stood in front of the school entrance and waved goodbye to her. He had insisted on taking his model of the Fokker D triplane to show his teacher. His mother recognized with bittersweet pain that an era had come to an end. When he waved, she fought the impulse to run to him and hold him. She had stood there and waved, smiling with the tears running down her cheeks.

From the time Jimmy was born, his parents had invested heavily in him. Their investment can be measured in hours and days, in care and planning—planning those little things that would make Jimmy happy. A rough indication of their investment can be seen in the number of projects Jimmy's father had undertaken with the boy, like the Fokker D project. Jimmy was the most precious boy in the world. And his parents had done everything the better books and magazine articles had instructed them to do with their child. They had purchased educational toys. They had seen to it that Jimmy had nutritious meals and that he had regular medical and dental checkups. They had engaged Jimmy in a great deal of informal instruction—the kind that was designed to make him ready for school. By all the traditional measures they had succeeded very well. Jimmy had been well prepared for kindergarten. He had a high IQ; he was extremely verbal; his capacity to learn was above average.

A Change in Jimmy

During Jimmy's first-grade year, his parents began to sense that something was wrong. Jimmy began to change. He didn't wolf his breakfast anymore and dash off to school. He began to say, "I don't feel good. I think I should stay home and rest."

His parents allowed him to stay home on a couple of occasions. But Jimmy continued to complain. One morning at breakfast his father said to him, "You've been pulling this quite a bit lately. You don't have a fever or a cold. You've got to go to school."

"Do I have to, Dad? I really don't feel very well."

"Jean, what the hell's wrong? What's going on in school?"

Jimmy's mother set up an appointment with Jimmy's teacher to try to find out. Jimmy's father stayed home from work that day and went along.

The young woman was in her first year of teaching and seemed somewhat ill at ease talking to Jimmy's parents. "Jimmy is a very, very smart boy," she said. "In fact, I would say that he contributes more to our class discussions than any other child."

"Why does he hate school lately?" his father asked. "Is he being tormented by some of the other children?"

"I don't believe anything is really happening," the teacher

said. "Jimmy is going through a period of adjustment. He's not reading and I think he is bothered by it."

"Jimmy not reading?" his father said. "He knew all the letters in the alphabet before he entered kindergarten. Why isn't he reading?"

"Children do things when they are ready," the teacher said. "We know that Jimmy has the ability—there's no question about that. When he works through his adjustment problem he will read. I just wouldn't worry about it."

"Is there anything that we can do to help him?" his mother asked.

"Yes, be patient."

"No, I meant specifically to help him with his reading," Jimmy's mother said.

The teacher thought a moment. "I don't think that it would be wise."

Jimmy's parents left the meeting with the feeling that nothing had really been settled. "We'll just have to wait and see," Jimmy's father said.

Learning to Accept Failure

They waited and they saw. They saw Jimmy's hatred of school grow. They didn't know that Jimmy could not work the written problems in his arithmetic workbook because he could not read them. Although he was very good at problems that were presented verbally, arithmetic was becoming a punishing subject. He would work the straight computation problems on his arithmetic worksheet, but he wouldn't try to work the other problems. He would hand in the worksheet, and when it came back it would have C's next to each of the computation problems, and X's next to the story problems. At the top of the page, scrawled in red, was a word that Jimmy had learned to read: "Poor."

Jimmy tried to identify words by remembering their shapes and by cueing on some of the letters, but he was quite confused by now. His teacher encouraged him to think about the context of each word. She had asked him many times, "Well, what *could* that word be?" She had unintentionally prompted him to view written words as conveyors of ideas, not merely of sounds. As a result, he made the typical mistake that disabled sight readers make, such as calling the word *pretty* "beautiful." When he saw the word *pretty,* he knew the idea conveyed by the word, but he didn't know the most fundamental rule about the code for written words, which is that the letters *p-r-e-t-t-y* are guides to the sounds that the word makes.

By March, Jimmy had been demoted to the lowest reading group, the C group. Everybody knew it was the lowest group. Most of the kids in his class could now read, some fairly well. However, Jimmy and the other kids in the C group couldn't.

Jimmy's first-grade teacher indicated that he was "just not ready to read." She also must have known that without the ability to read instructions Jimmy couldn't possibly perform in second-grade activities. Yet she promoted him to second grade. The school endorsed the idea of "social promotions." The principal, Mr. Morris, put it somewhat unoriginally, saying, "It's important for children to feel as if they are succeeding. They should remain with their peers for their social growth. It's disturbing to children when they fail." Even though Jimmy moved to a second-grade classroom, he had failed and he was disturbed. He now regularly resisted going to school. He would leave in plenty of time to get to school, but he would arrive late.

"We'll have to punish you if you keep this up, Jimmy," his father would say.

"I don't like school," Jimmy would say. "I don't want to go there."

Jimmy's allowance was cut off, and he spent some Saturday afternoons in his room "studying." Both of his parents yelled at him with increasing frequency. From time to time, his father would have a heart-to-heart talk with him to try to capture the kind of relationship they used to have. "Look, Jimmy. We're concerned because we love you. Maybe we've been too hard on you.

Tell you what: let's set up the HO train set this Saturday. What do you say?"

"Okay, Dad." And for a while things were pleasant. On Monday morning the nightmare would begin—trying to get Jimmy out of bed, arguing with him about going to school, almost pushing him out the door.

During the middle of his second-grade year, Jimmy learned a new kind of reading behavior. He formulated a percentage game. He looked at the beginning of the word and thought of two or three possibilities. He then "read" the word hesitantly, saying the first possibility and looking at the teacher to see if she accepted his interpretation. If the teacher said nothing and didn't look up he would go to the next word. If she looked up or indicated in any way that his interpretation was incorrect, Jimmy would quickly say the second possibility, trying to convey the idea that he had experienced a momentary lapse. He did this by hitting himself on the side of the head and saying, "I mean . . ." before saying the second choice.

Jimmy's second-grade teacher was not convinced that he would read when he was ready. She had seen Jimmys before; she recognized their symptoms and she knew that they were disabled. The teacher called for help. Ironically, Mary answered the call. She began working with Jimmy twice a week. In the meantime, Jimmy's teacher had to fit Jimmy into the school instruction as well as she could. The readers used in her second grade were part of the same Bill-and-Sally series used in the first grade. Jimmy sat in on a reading group every day with his classroom teacher as they went through the first-grade primers that Jimmy had more or less memorized the preceding year.

Jimmy was now officially termed a reading problem. Reading problems are usually taught phonics after they have failed with the look-and-guess approach. On two days a week, Jimmy studied phonics, learning the sounds that the letters make and phonic rules: when there is an *e* on the end of the word, the preceding vowel is long if it is followed by a single consonant. Jimmy learned to recite the rule, but he never learned how to apply it.

It became a ritual. When Jimmy had trouble with the word *gave,* Mary would ask him the rule about the final *e*. Jimmy would recite the rule, then try to sound out the word. "Jimmy, you're not making the *a* long. *Ayyyy.* Make it long." After Mary had demonstrated the sound, Jimmy could apply the rule. Mary wondered why a boy as intelligent as Jimmy could have so much trouble applying these rules. She apparently didn't realize that the rule means little if the child is not familiar with examples that fit the rules. For Jimmy, all words were signals for him to become anxious. He would sometimes remember all of the wrong responses that he had made in the past. "Don't call that word *he*," he would say to himself. "Don't call it *and.* Don't call it . . ." He couldn't remember consistently to call it *the*. It didn't help much when Mary explained that it began with *th*. Letters convey sounds, but a word that begins with *th* doesn't convey the sound *t*. It conveys the sound . . . what is that word?

Jimmy learned to recite many rules: the one about vowels walking together while one talks and the other one walks; the one about *ou* and the sound it makes; the one about prefixes. Mary wasn't completely aware of the paradox Jimmy presented. The rules were supposed to help him develop the behavior of reading words like *meat, boat, this, gave,* and *out*. Jimmy knew the rules, but he wasn't developing the behavior.

The Label of Failure

By the middle of the second grade, Jimmy had developed a new two-step approach for attacking words. He first took a shot at the word, keeping in mind some of the other possibilities. If his guess didn't work, he quickly tried his second possibility. Usually, Mary would stop him at this point and have him sound out the word. Most of the time he would identify the word after sounding it out. Jimmy had seen his classmates read a "faster way" than sounding out. So Jimmy tended to revert to his guessing. Since his guesses were right at least half of the time, this method was reinforced. "Maybe I'll get it this time," Jimmy thought somewhat optimistically.

By the end of his second-grade year, Jimmy was functionally a nonreader. The school system seemed to be more than justified in officially labeling Jimmy a "specific learning disability."

This label is supposed to signify a strange intellectual-growth pattern. According to the traditional interpretation, a child with an IQ of 100, which is normal or average, is supposed to progress in reading at a normal or average rate. A child with an IQ above 100 is supposed to progress at an above-average rate, while the kid with the IQ lower than 100 moves at a slower-than-normal rate. A specific learning disability exhibits a discrepancy between his IQ score and his reading ability. There are some complicated formulas, such as the Tinker-Bond formula, for determining whether a child fits into the learning-disability category. Jimmy definitely fit by any formula. According to his IQ, ostensibly the measure of his capacity, he should have been a superior reader. His actual reading performance, however, was about the same as that of a child with an 80 IQ. (Note that a nonreading child with an 80 IQ is not considered a freak. He is not a specific learning disability. He is expected to read below normal, and teachers aren't supposed to worry about his poor performance. If this child weren't a reading failure, he would be a freak in the traditional scheme.)

If a child scores high on an IQ test and goes through the reading program with no difficulties, the child both has the capacity to learn, according to the traditional interpretation, and has been made "ready." However, this child may fail in school. The schools could say, "Maybe our predictors—the IQ and the readiness program—are not very good at predicting failure; therefore, we should scrap them." Or they could say, "The kid was perfectly ready and we failed to teach him; therefore, our methods of instruction leave something to be desired."

Typically, the schools don't use either explanation. Instead, they label the child "specific learning disability," implying that there is something wrong with *him*. His failure is evidence that he has a deficiency that was responsible for his failure.

As absurd as the label of specific learning disability is, it is frighteningly common, particularly in affluent school districts. There are classrooms of capable children in which perhaps one third receive the distinction of becoming learning disabilities. In some cities, the label is so common that it is vogueish for parents to take the child to a clinic, where they spend a great deal of money and perhaps accumulate a few more labels for their child. The child is not "cured" of his dyslexia or his learning disability through the clinic, but the parent has a great deal to discuss at cocktail parties.

Even more frightening is the implication that the child who is labeled a specific learning disability would have developed problems regardless of the instruction he received. The label is more than a catch-all. It is the quintessence of the school's resistance to admitting that it is accountable for the child's performance. If all other labels are inappropriate and if the child passes all of the screening tests used to assess readiness and capacity, sock him with the specific-disability label.

The Null Approach

When we look at the instruction Jimmy received, however, we notice that what he learned was perfectly consistent with what his teachers did when they tried to instruct him. Jimmy learned to "make up" stories about the pictures, but every demonstration of "reading" he received was consistent with the interpretation that reading involves making up such narrations. He failed to learn that the letter sounds make the sound of the word, but his teacher encouraged him to guess at words, to use context cues and to look at the pictures.

Furthermore, the basal series that Jimmy used obscured the relationship between symbol and sound. Within the first week of instruction Jimmy had encountered the letter *o* in these words: *to, do, go, mother, come, for,* and *you.* The first words containing the letter *e* were these: *she, the, mother, come, ride, gave,* and *eat.* It is understandable that Jimmy got the impression that the letters had little to do with the sounds one said when pronouncing the words. The letter *o* makes five different sounds; *e* makes three and doesn't make any apparent sound in three of the words.

The case for the label of specific learning disability is factually weak. It has a great convenience appeal, however, in that it leads to a null approach, or an approach that involves limited professional skill. It would take a concerted teaching effort to change Jimmy's behavior by the time he reaches the fifth grade and has had five years to practice his confused decoding strategy. The label of specific disability does not imply such an effort. The child has something wrong with him. No particular instruction is implied.

Nearly all of the educational approaches that have become popular and received great publicity over the past ten years have been null approaches that imply very limited professional skill on the part of the teacher. Consider discovery learning. The teacher may be instructed by her teacher's guide not to give the children the answers to any of the exercises. According to the guide, the children are to discover on their own, and "they will discover when they are ready." This orientation places the most limited professional responsibility on the teacher.

An interesting, but not surprising, fact about discovery learning is that in most studies in which the discovery approach is compared with even the most unenlightened-schoolmarm traditional approach, the discovery approach comes out a poor second. Yet educators find it appealing, because it is a null approach.

Consider such approaches as the much publicized "talking typewriter." The children are supposed to learn to read by experimenting with a rigged typewriter that permits them to type only certain words or combinations. The approach became popular (if not widely implemented) before there were any data to suggest that it worked. Again, the appeal lies in the nullness of the approach. The children are responsible for their own learning. If learning doesn't happen with some children, the traditional educator concludes that they probably weren't ready.

Individualized instruction, as it is generally implemented, is a null approach. The most popular individualized reading program for young children does not work with a large percentage of the children. Several studies have disclosed that some children can go through the "programmed" exercises, in which the children make marks on a paper, without learning how to read. Other individualized programs such as the foreign-language learning with headphones and records have proved to be enormously inferior to approaches in which a teacher drills children on sentences in a foreign language. Yet the records and headphones require far less professional responsibility.

The null approach applies to teachers as well as children. This point can be illustrated by a research study of a few years ago in which the investigator ostensibly demonstrated that teacher expectations influence children's performance. He told teachers that specific children in their classes were latent learners and would soon blossom. The children identified as latent learners were randomly selected. At the end of the year, national news services reported the investigator's findings that the "latent" learners progressed more than the other children. The investigator received a professorial appointment at Harvard. It wasn't until his study became the rage of the educational world that other investigators examined his data and discovered that it was a mess, that the teachers didn't consistently remember which children had been identified as latent learners, and that the study did not give very strong support to the idea that unprofessional expectations have a salutary effect on the children's performance.

Why was the educational world so quick to accept the study? I submit that its appeal had to do with the implied null approach. Think of how wonderfully simple teacher training would be if the study were valid. You could give teachers a quick Dale Carnegie course and stimulate them to think positively. From then on, everything would take care of itself, just like magic.

The open classroom, where the child is supposed to choose those activities that are most appropriate for his inner needs and his developmental level, is one of the currently popular examples of a null approach. If a child wants to hammer on a block all day for weeks, that's all right, according to the more extreme advocate, because "when he's ready, he will become interested in reading." Again, the data do not support the contention that the open classroom produces instructional outcomes that are even as impressive as the kind of traditional approach that Mary uses. Some advocates of the program argue that academic performance is not important and that the social development of the children is fostered better in the open classroom. There are no data to support this contention. The approach is popular because, like discovery learning, it places responsibility for learning on the child, not on the teacher or the system. The teacher's role is restricted to that of an observer and encourager.

Finally, consider the highly debated educational plan of busing minority children. Why did it become so popular? It implies no professional responsibility. Aside from the "social" and legal issues involved, the assumption seems to be that we have discharged our obligation to Andy when we allow him to spend two hours a day on a bus that takes him across town. There are no provisions for teaching him once he arrives at his destination; yet it is a lot easier (and probably more expensive) to bus than it is to teach.

The traditional educator espouses the idea of social promotions, in which the child is required to perform in material that is more difficult than the material he failed to master in the lower grade, even though there is no logical way that a child can handle complicated comprehension items if he hasn't mastered simple ones. There are probably few situations more punishing to a child than one in which he receives a continual demonstration that others in the class can perform in the academic material that he cannot handle. The demonstration of his incompetence is so compelling that it is doubtful that the child will be able to maintain a "positive self-image." Social promotions do not involve professional skill. Perhaps that's why they're popular.

Make No Mystique

Teaching, as we indicated earlier, is the manipulation of environmental variables to cause specific behavioral changes in the child. When we describe a child like Jimmy, we must describe him so that *teaching* is implied. If we talk about his learning disability or his learning capacity, no teaching is implied; the problem is quite clearly Jimmy's, not the teacher's. Therefore, we can't refer to learning. On the other hand, if we say, "Jimmy hasn't been taught the following skills," and list them, teaching is implied. By using this description, we acknowledge the problem; however, we don't place a stigma on Jimmy. We are merely indicating the skills he has not been taught.

This approach has been rejected by traditional educational theorists, perhaps because it is possible to describe a child in many different ways. We can view him as a genetic creature, a biological entity, a network of atoms, a learning thing, a social being, an interacting organism, a developing and growing thing. We can identify needs, interests, desires, activities, states. We can look at him physically, mentally, emotionally, transcendentally. But should we? The answer is that all depends on what you plan to do with him. If you plan to watch him, categorize him, or note patterns of interaction, these descriptions are splendid. If you plan to teach him, however, you'd better follow the lead of professionals in other fields and limit your description to those aspects of the child that are consistent with the role of the practitioner. A teacher, the practitioner, must manipulate environmental variables. Any description, regardless of how "true," "observable," or just plain compelling it may be, must be rejected by the teacher *if it does not imply manipulation of environmental variables.* In other words, the description must imply teaching.

Anybody would be intellectually sterile if he couldn't make the observation that Andy lacks "aptitude," or that Jimmy has a learning problem of some sort. Yet when a teacher is functioning in her professional role, she must reject the idea of aptitude, because aptitude does not imply teaching. Merely because aptitude is observable does not mean that it should be allowed as a professionally acceptable statement.

When a teacher sits down with a child, she will do things, no matter how hard she tries not to. In other words, she will manipulate environmental variables. She therefore must work from a description of the child that gives her guidelines about what to do. The only such description is one that refers to what the child has and what he hasn't been taught. If the teacher knows that Jimmy hasn't been taught specific skills, the implication is rather direct and simple: teach him. However, if the teacher accepts any other description of the child, such as aptitude, no clear guidelines are provided. It is not clear how to change a child's aptitude through manipulation of environmental variables.

Most of the cherished descriptions of traditional education must be rejected for the same reason that aptitude is rejected. Describing Andy in terms of his past history is not allowable. There is no way that a teacher can take him back to birth and give him a different history. She can only teach him.

Another sacrosanct description has to do with the current home situation. Let's say that things are bad at home. Other agencies may be quite interested in such a statement, since they deal with solutions to home problems. The teacher, however, does not deal with these problems.

Although the idea of restricting descriptions of the child to terms that are consistent with the act of teaching is viewed as very extreme by traditional educators, it seems far more extreme to hope that if the teacher is provided with a full list of true statements about a child she will know more about teaching him. She'll probably get lost somewhere between his past history, his IQ, and his "needs," and probably use the descriptions not as a foundation for designing instruction but to serve as excuses for providing a null approach. By using the traditional descriptions, we can find reasons why any child who is six years old should fail in school. The child probably had at least one high fever or severe head bump. He probably experienced some toilet-training problems. His history may disclose more than a hint of sibling rivalry or of fear of the dark. We could discover that he spent too much time on physical activities or on mental activities, too much time unsupervised or not enough. If he happened to come out perfectly average on all measures, he would indeed be the object of great suspicion, because practically no child is average on all measures.

These descriptions provide no pertinent information about the child, at least from a teaching standpoint. The child exhibits certain behavior or he doesn't. If he doesn't, it really doesn't matter how the problem originated. Nor does it matter what other interesting things may have happened in the child's life. What matters is his present behavior, because that is all the teacher observes or works with.

A Slow Change

The picture that I have painted in this chapter is grim and may convey the impression that every teacher and every school system is guilty of playing the labeling game to cover up failures. Actually, there is a movement to abolish spurious labels and deal with the actual problems of instruction. Some states, such as California, have taken at least the first steps required to do away with custodial classrooms for the labeled child. Oregon, Virginia, and a few other states have adopted legislation that requires the teaching of basic "survival skills" to children. There is a great deal of discussion in educational circles about "criterion-referenced" tests, which are tests designed to document whether the children have mastered that which is taught in school. And a number of educators and psychologists have conducted a concerted battle against the use of labels that don't imply teaching. At the New York Academy of Sciences' 1972 Conference on Minimal Brain Dysfunction, two of the papers delivered departed radically from the traditional line. One by Alan Cohen, professor of education at Yeshiva University, was titled "Minimal Brain Dysfunction and Practical Matters Such as Teaching Kids to Read," and argued that traditional labels function as a hindrance to effective instruction. The second paper, written by Barbara Bateman, professor of special education at the University of Oregon, showed how absurd the kind of logic used by traditional theorists would be if it were applied to a practical situation, such as diagnosing the problems of a car that breaks down on the highway. The last sentence of the paper is: "No, Virginia, a diagnosis of MBD [minimal brain dysfunction] does not help an educator start the car." (An interesting aside is that the label of MBD was invented not by psychologists but by the manufacturer of a tranquilizer.)

We could add many names to the list of those who are calling for reform in the school's attitude toward the school failure and in the role of the school in protecting against such failure. In actual practice, however, there has been very little change in what happens in the typical school.

Go to nearly any junior high or high school and you will see a frighteningly high percentage of Jimmys. Their behavior hasn't changed appreciably since the third grade, except that most of them are now *confirmed* behavior problems. They read with the same kind of errors that Jimmy makes. They reverse, read synonyms, omit words, confuse words such as *when/then, what/that*. They know tricks for getting kicked out of the social-studies class, the science class, and any other academic class they have. And the fact that they are "failures" has been demonstrated to them frequently.

In a study on teacher–child interactions reported by Hill Walker, the number of disapproving comments gives an indication of how forceful these failure demonstrations are. Teachers were disapproving in almost ninety percent of their interactions. In another study, Walker noted that one teacher averaged 182 disapproving comments a day, compared with an average of 12 approving comments. The preponderance of negative comments (disapproval) holds even for teachers who are not considered punitive. It should come as no particular surprise that their kids are turned off. Who wouldn't be?

On the first-grade level, there is ample evidence that the unfounded-labeling game is continuing in full force. Rodney is a typical victim. In the fall of 1973, he was quite similar to the Jimmy who entered the second grade. Rodney had been labeled so convincingly that his mother's hopes were modest about correcting his problems. He was seven years old. Before I saw the boy, I asked his mother if he could repeat simple statements such as "The dog jumped over the fence." She replied, "Of course," and added a puzzled look, which turned skeptical when I said that, sight unseen, we would teach that kid to read before Christmas.

Within two weeks he had mastered about one year's worth of reading skills. The instruction was provided by one of the teacher trainers on our staff. After tutoring him for an hour on her first day, she asked me, "Are you sure we've got the right kid? He's covered over twelve lessons so far." Rodney is probably an extreme example, but he's quite real. And if some strong intervention had not been provided when it was provided, Rodney probably would have joined those kids in the junior high who have learned to live with their labels and to accept school as an alien agency that offers them little hope and less reinforcement.

4

Behavior

Manipulating Human Beings

Our description of teaching refers to causing behavioral changes and manipulating things. These references are red flags to many educators. They hold that the manipulation of children conflicts with humanistic goals, that it smacks of mechanism, divests the child of his right to freedom, and reduces him to the status of a pawn that is controlled à la 1984.

Their position stems from a thorough misunderstanding of the situation. The choice is not between manipulating children and not manipulating them. The choice is between doing those things that will produce the desired effects and doing those that will fail. Nearly everybody agrees that we want our children to be creative, capable of making intelligent decisions, capable of discovering, questioning, and analyzing. We want our kids to function independently, work for rewards that are intrinsic in the activities they pursue, and exhibit positive attitudes toward school activities. The question is, how do we get them to that point? We have basically two choices. We can ignore the principles that would direct us to the systematic realization of those goals. Or we can say that we are not manipulating children while we unintentionally manipulate them and cause undesired behaviors.

We can illustrate the difference between careful manipulation and unintentional manipulation by looking at two groups of children who have been labeled severely disturbed.

We'll first visit a traditional institution where the prevailing philosophy is that the children are suffering from some illness which has its roots in an emotional trauma experienced by the child in the past. The child's behavior, on the other hand, is treated as a mere symptom of the child's emotional disease.

Our guide is Dr. James, a recognized authority on dealing with severely disturbed and autistic children. On the way to a classroom he explains, "The children in this class are severe cases. We are making progress with some of them. But others . . ."

As we walk into the room we notice that a teacher is wrestling a large wooden block from a child who looks about ten years old. When she sees us she stops and says, "Be careful with that block," and combs the child's hair with her fingers.

The child pulls away and runs across the room.

A young boy runs up to us. "Fuck you," he says. "Fuck you."

Dr. James smiles faintly.

A teacher and an aide are attempting to work with about ten children, although the nature of the activity is not obvious. A tall girl who has been sitting on the floor in the back of the room stands up and viciously hits a little blond boy. The aide and the teacher rush over and try to pull the girl away. The girl screams, "You son of a bitch, take your hands off me!"

"We have to let the children act out their aggressions, at the same time keeping them from injuring one another," Dr. James explains.

"Why do you want them to act out their aggressions?" we ask.

The doctor looks shocked. "Why? . . . Well, if the children

aren't allowed to act out their aggressions, they'll continue to be emotionally disturbed."

"Says who?" we ask.

"It's a well-known medical fact that these children's pent-up aggressions must be released and rechanneled."

A fat girl falls onto the floor and starts babbling. The aide rushes over to comfort her.

"Why did that girl throw a tantrum?" we ask.

"She was probably confronted with some frustration that she was unable to handle. She is probably afraid of her own feelings and, being unable to face them, she explodes into a tantrum."

"Does the aide or teacher give that girl attention every time she throws a tantrum?"

"Yes. We want her to learn that her feelings are natural and that we will not reject her because she has these feelings."

"Isn't it possible that the child has been unintentionally taught that she can get attention by throwing a tantrum?"

"I hardly think that such is the case," replied Dr. James.

The boy who greeted us with "Fuck you" didn't come to the institution two years before with that behavior. Through activities that were intended to do something else, he was taught that ploy for getting a rise out of visitors. Since coming to the institution he hasn't learned to read. He hasn't been taught the meaning of the words *yes* and *no*. He is still confused over the words *me, you, your, mine*. He has, however, been taught some advanced techniques about controlling adults by acting in bizarre ways.

Our second stop is a classroom in a public school. The teacher does not espouse the medical-model philosophy that the child's behavior is a symptom of deep-seated disease. Her motto is that a child is not labeled emotionally disturbed if he doesn't exhibit emotionally disturbed behavior. Her goal is to eliminate the children's emotionally disturbed behavior and replace it with appropriate behavior, thus making the children appear "normal."

The teacher is working with five children, while the other

eight are at their desks, working on sheets of arithmetic problems. We observe no tantrums, no children running around the room. The teacher says to the group of five children, "The last problem for today is *tough*. I don't think you'll be able to work it."

"Yes, we can," the children say.

"Let's see." The teacher writes on the board:

$$5 + \square = 8$$

"Work this problem on your fingers. Raise your hand when you know the answer."

We can hear several children count as they hold up each finger, "Six, seven, eight." All hands go up.

"George, what's the answer?"

"We had to plus three."

"Is that right?" the teacher says with mock disbelief.

"Yes, that's right," a girl on the end of the group says, standing up.

"That's right," chime the others.

"No, no," the teacher says. "That's not right and I can prove it." She points to the 8. "We have eight on this side of the equal, so we have to have eight on the other side. But I only see five on that side. So we have to plus. We have five, so I get it going. Fiiiiiivvve." The teacher then counts, holding up a finger every time she counts, "Six, seven, eight."

She smiles, holding up the three fingers. "You said that we had to plus three. But look at how many we really had to plus—" Her face falls. The children laugh.

"We were right," they say.

The teacher says, "You're getting too smart for me. You worked so hard, I'm going to have to give you each five points. And I only get two points."

The children beam.

"Okay, back to your seats," the teacher says. "Let's see how well the others have been working. I'll bet nobody finished two sheets of problems."

"I finished *four*," one of the boys announces from his seat.

"So did I," a little black girl says.

"I'm on my fourth one now," says another girl.

The teacher examines each child's work and makes comments like "I didn't know you were that smart" and "If you get much smarter, I won't be able to teach you anything."

The teacher awards points to all of the children.

Then the children go to the "store," a cabinet filled with toys and goodies like potato chips and candy bars. Each item is worth so many points. The children purchase what they want with the points they have accumulated.

This teacher succeeded with the same kind of children that we observed in the other institution, because the kind of therapy she provides is effective both in controlling "emotional" problems and in educating the children. She managed to teach her children at the rate of the *average-to-smart* child.

Dr. James has launched vicious attacks against those who would manipulate children, bribe them with rewards, and work only with the symptoms and not the causes of the emotional diseases. The evidence is strongly against Dr. James, however. He has never actually cured a child. If anything, he has exaggerated the very maladaptive behaviors he tried to change. The classroom teacher, on the other hand, has an impressive batting average. Most of the children she gets look pretty good after half a year. Some of the others take longer, and she fails with about one out of every twenty.

You may wonder why Dr. James would be dedicated to the kind of program that obviously doesn't work. B. F. Skinner may have provided the answer in *The Technology of Teaching:*

> We fear effective teaching, as we fear all effective means of changing human behavior. Power not only corrupts, it frightens; and absolute power frightens absolutely. . . . It could well be that a technology of teaching will be unwisely used. It could destroy initiative and creativity; it could make men all alike (and not necessarily in being equally excellent); it could sup-

press the beneficial effect of accidents on the development of the individual and on the evolution of a culture. On the other hand, it could maximize the genetic endowment of each student; it could make him as skillful, competent, and informed as possible; it could build the greatest diversity of interests; it could lead him to make the greatest possible contribution to the survival and development of his cult ᵌ. Which of these futures lies before us will not be determined by the mere availability of effective instruction. The use to which a technology of teaching is to be put will depend upon other matters.

I was witness to an incredible example of the fear to which Skinner refers. A few years ago a professor who is now dean of the college of education at one of the leading Midwest universities visited the preschool for disadvantaged children that Carl Bereiter and I were operating at the University of Illinois. After his visit, he explained that he was philosophically disturbed by what he had observed. He indicated that he had expected to see little robotlike children being punished and drilled in dull academic skills. Instead, he saw five-year-olds who were generally happy, obviously proud, and performing quite well in arithmetic, reading, and language.

Several days later, he returned and announced that he had figured out what bothered him. "It works. That's what bothers me. It really works."

Bereiter and I asked him to explain what he meant. He said, "I can't help but think what would happen if these techniques got into the hands of the wrong people. They could turn children into monsters. I feel that we are better off with techniques that are not effective, because we wouldn't run the risk of those techniques being used by the wrong people."

We pointed out that his argument was absurd. Any profession—medical, legal, engineering—has powerful techniques that work. What if these techniques got into the hands of the wrong people? On the other hand, if we removed the powerful techniques from these professions and used only innocuous ones, the professions would be reduced to debating societies.

The professor was not convinced by our arguments. In 1970, when he became dean of the college of education, he wrote in his acceptance speech, "In spite of the turmoil, and in spite of the increasing suspicion about the ability of the scholarly community to be responsive, we stand to receive a disproportionate share of the resources that may be made available for higher education if we can help to chart some paths out of our current educational dilemmas—or at least show that we really know the problems are severe, and that we care!"

Dr. James and the members of his staff care. They understand the severity of the problem. Unfortunately, caring and understanding are not quite enough. The professional must have powerful tools and use them effectively if he is to chart paths out of the educational dilemma.

The Technology of Choices: Operant Conditioning

Some powerful behavioral techniques were introduced in classrooms and institutions in 1964. These techniques (the kind used by the classroom teacher we visited) were based on the theory of operant conditioning developed by Skinner and others. They added a new ingredient to the core that had been the traditional diet for the disturbed child. And they worked.

The operant-conditioning theory provides principles for changing behavior. One such principle is that children will work harder if they receive a reward for their efforts. This principle and the others articulated in the theory are based on evidence and seem quite consistent with situations that every adult has observed many times. Nevertheless, operant conditioning has been the subject of heated debate. The reason probably is that those who oppose it react to the name, particularly the "conditioning" part. This word apparently evokes the image of a Pavlovian reflex action.

Operant conditioning has nothing to do with reflexes, but applies to situations where the organism has a choice of actions or responses that it can produce. This difference is very important. A child who is told to do his arithmetic worksheet has choices. He can either do the worksheet, look out the window, draw a picture, or belt the little girl sitting next to him. Operant psychology would hold that if you want the child to choose one of these actions over the others, *you have to make that one more rewarding (or less punishing) than the others.* The value in making the desired activity rewarding (rather than less punishing) is that if the child learns that working arithmetic problems is "rewarding" he will tend to work on arithmetic problems even when he is not rewarded. If he is taught that every time he doesn't do his artithmetic problems he gets clobbered, he will learn a great deal about what happens when he doesn't do arithmetic, but very little about the rewards that may be associated with doing arithmetic.

Give the kid a reason for doing what you want him to do. Set up a contingency so that if he performs he receives something that he wants. The only way he can get the payoff is to do what you want him to do.

Some children do not work for the joy of doing arithmetic. By using payoffs to get them started, the teacher can systematically build up "motivation." At first the child is interested only in the specific payoff—the candy or the extra recess. As he learns, he receives other payoffs, such as praise for good work. After a while he learns to treat the payoff more as a symbol of his competence than as an end in itself. And he learns that the work itself was perhaps less than fun but certainly not punishment. Finally the child will be willing to work for nothing more than the praise and sense of achievement associated with performing well. Although the payoff principle is sometimes viewed as dehumanizing and mechanistic, it says in effect to the child, "I accept you where you are; I don't care how badly the past has treated you. I don't care how miserably your home or school has failed to teach you skills and work habits. I will find the payoffs that *you* are willing to work for. And I will take you, a step at a time, from where you are until you learn to read for the joy that one finds in reading and until you learn to perform well for the sense of pride that one experiences when he knows that he has performed well."

What Is Intrinsic Motivation?

One objection of some educators to the use of payoffs or rewards is that those rewards are extrinsic and children should be intrinsically motivated. The definition of intrinsic motivation is rarely provided. If it means that the child has a motive to read, I hope I never see such a child. He would devour the telephone directory with the same vigor with which he would attack *Bambi,* because the reading material (which is extrinsic) could not control his motives. On the other hand, if the "intrinsically motivated" child is one who prefers *Bambi* over the telephone directory because he finds *Bambi* rewarding, the "intrinsically motivated" child is what operant conditioning is all about. He is responding to rewards. For him, the reward is not a piece of candy or an encouraging word from the teacher. It is the content of *Bambi.* Ultimately, we want children to respond to such rewards. But precisely how do we get the child to this stage of performance?

Look at the child who is learning how to read. With great effort and concentration, he struggles through such passages as "Pam had a pan. The pan that Pam had is tan." The potential content rewards that derive from this passage are probably not much greater than those in the phone directory. What, then, will motivate the child? The feeling that he is accomplishing something important and that the teacher will acknowledge the effort that he extends in reading the passage. "Good job, Tom."

When the child is reading on the level of Pam and "See Dick run" we have these choices. We can refuse to work with the child who does not work for the joy of the task, or we can build a bridge and introduce other rewards that will stimulate him to read and practice until he reaches the point at which his skills are sufficiently developed for him to become hooked on the content of what he reads.

The Learning Center at Fort Meade

The traditional educator often does not accept the possibility that a child may not come into the classroom with wide-eyed eagerness to learn. The reason may be that the educator doesn't view the "indifferent" or lazy child as his responsibility. For this child the school often becomes punishing. The child's initial indifference to academic learning becomes active resistance, and the child is labeled. Now the child is often subjected to techniques that are supposed to be appropriate for the disturbed child. The results, like those of Dr. James, are often an intensification of the behaviors that are maladaptive.

By using appropriate operant techniques, the incorrigible behavior will change. The extent to which this can be done has been demonstrated by the learning center at Fort Meade, Maryland. The center is a cooperative venture between the Ann Arundel School District (with over fifty thousand students) and Behavioral Services Consultants, a nonprofit corporation. The learning center, housed in a group of dilapidated buildings at Fort Meade, serves a group of high-school-age incorrigibles who were judged too wild to continue in the public schools.

The school's format is a variation of the "open classroom." The kids are not required to go to classes. They may stay in the "rest" area, but if they want to earn "points" they must go into the classroom and work on academic skills. These points can be used to go to the recreation area, to purchase treats, or to go on special trips. A good-work-week letter is sent to the parents of the child who earns a certain number of points.

If the child does not respond to the payoffs that are available in school, the staff attempts to make a contract between the parents and the child. Since the usual payoff used by parents to reinforce good performance is money, the usual contract stipulates that if the child completes so many units during the school week, he will earn so much money.

These kids are well-behaved—without guards or any form of suppression. There are virtually no fights at the school. The academic progress of many students is five times the rate they had been taught in the public schools.

Let's visit the barracks in which reading is taught. Forty kids are seated at tables or browsing through books on the shelves. Nearly all of them are on individual programs. The teacher is working with a sixteen-year-old white boy who is reading a third-grade story. After he finishes a chapter, the teacher assigns two or three words that the boy missed. She then gives him credit for a "unit," which means that the boy has earned points. As the boy fills out the form that the teacher must sign, the teacher tells us, "Ralph has been doing as many as five lessons a day. He couldn't read a word in October." Ralph looks up and smiles.

As the teacher walks into the next room, where two boys are waiting to have their work checked, she says, "We have a tremendous range. Some of the kids can read very well, perhaps on ninth-grade level or better. At the beginning of the year they ranged all the way down to nonreaders. Now they can all read."

The teacher checks a black boy who reads from a fifth-grade book. He makes quite a few mistakes. The teacher informs us that the boy started the year reading on perhaps the beginning-second-grade level. As she talks to us, several boys start to clown around. She puts her hand on one boy's shoulder. "Come on, Henry, cut it out," she says quietly. Henry smiles and sits down.

Some children seem quite pleased with their accomplishments. Others don't show how they feel, but they are there, reading, evidence that they find reading instruction reinforcing.

We go across the "campus" to another barracks, where arithmetic is taught and where the principal, Mr. Brown, has his office. Just as we start to chat with him, one of the boys sticks his head in the door. "Mr. Brown," he says, "why don't you take me out to lunch sometime?"

"Whoa," Mr. Brown says. "I'm getting tired of doing things for you. When are you going to do something for *me?*"

"What do you want me to do?"

"I'd like to see you get a good-work-week letter this week."

"I already got sixty points this week."

"Then it shouldn't be hard for you to get the letter."

The boy smiles. "If I get a good-work-week letter will you take me to McDonald's?"

"Sure."

"All right," the boy says and claps his hands.

"Wait a minute," Mr. Brown says, "I'll take you to McDonald's if you earn a good-work-week letter, but what are you going to do to reward me for my good behavior?"

"What do you mean?"

"When I take you to McDonald's I'm being nice to you, right? Well, what are you going to do to reward me for being nice?"

The boy shrugs.

"I'll tell you what," Mr. Brown says. "You can reward me by doing three extra units in arithmetic. Fair enough?"

The boy ponders for a moment. "Okay."

"Write up the contract," Mr. Brown says, "and I'll sign it. Have you got it straight?"

"I get it," the boy replies. "I get a good-work-week letter and you'll take me to McDonald's. You take me to McDonald's and I'll do three extra units in arithmetic."

"Right."

After the boy ducks out the door, Mr. Brown laughs and says, "That boy has a psychological record as long as your arm.

They were going to put him away. Now he's doing beautifully. His folks moved to Baltimore two months ago. He comes here every day, even though it's a long drive. We're going to have to put him back into regular school. I just hope that . . ." Mr. Brown's voice trails off.

Brown tells about the school, how it has changed, the things that the staff still has to work on. We leave his office and watch kids in arithmetic class doing from third- to tenth-grade work. None seems to mind when we look over his shoulder.

Outside the barracks, we observe a group of boys planting bushes to make the place more attractive. As we watch them, we can appreciate the message of operant conditioning. These kids were incorrigible because incorrigible behavior was a natural reaction to the punishing situations in which they had been placed. The same incorrigible kids look quite different if the situation is changed so that they can succeed and receive some satisfaction or "reward" for succeeding.

Learning to Do What's Unnatural

If a teacher is to achieve the type of results observed at the learning center, she must change the punishing situation. A large part of the change involves her behavior. To be effective, she must forget the instruction she probably received in college about behaving in a manner that is natural, and learn to behave in ways that may be quite unnatural. Regardless of how unnatural the new behaviors may be, they will work, a phenomenon that was illustrated in a study by Wesley Becker. The investigator worked with a teacher of "severely disturbed" kids. The teacher didn't set things up so that the children could succeed. She never paid off children who were performing well. Instead, she gave attention to children who misbehaved. When the study began, kids were yelling, biting, shouting. Above the din, you could scarcely hear the teacher's "All right. Sit down. Mark, sit down. That goes for you too, Davy!" Her manner was reminiscent of a top sergeant's. But the kids didn't respond. At the end of the day the teacher was disgusted. She had spent most of the day failing to get all of the kids even to sit down, let alone open a textbook or try to study. On the average, the kids were off task over seventy percent of the instructional time.

Becker's experiment was simple. The teacher was given instructions about praising children when they did something well and ignoring them when they were disruptive. She was to ignore Mark, who was throwing paper, and praise Silas, who was doing his work. The point that the investigator hoped to demonstrate was that the children's behavior would change *if the teacher's behavior changed.* If the teacher effectively praised those children who were performing well, the children's on-task performance would improve and their off-task behavior would diminish.

The investigator encountered one problem rather early in the experiment. The teacher just couldn't praise children. It wasn't that she felt unnatural praising children for doing a good job; *she couldn't do it.* Her first attempts, after some coaching, came out with barbs. When a child finished a worksheet, she would say something like "Very good, John, for a change!"

After more training, the teacher moved from barbed to phony praise. Jumping out of character, she would recite a stereotyped comment such as "Very, very good." Her attempts at praise were so unconvincing that the data collectors frequently noted in their logs "Phony praise" and "Nobody would believe this." Yet even during this period the deviant behavior of the children dropped from seventy percent to little more than thirty percent. That change in the children's behavior occurred when the teacher stopped doing what was natural for her and began using a technique that worked, even though this technique was quite unnatural. After several months, praise came naturally to the teacher.

Two important points emerge from this experiment. The first is that techniques work regardless of one's inner beliefs, motivation, or spirit. The second point is that the formula for succeeding in managing children is to structure the situation so that you're not giving all your attention to the children who act up. The principle is obvious. Executing it is not always as easy.

The Art Period

A few years ago, we were operating an experimental preschool at the University of Illinois. One of the newer trainers on our staff, a young artist named Patricia, felt that our curriculum was lacking in art experiences. We agreed. Patricia suggested that she take over one of the free periods and listed some of the things she wanted to do. The program sounded very interesting. When we asked her how she planned to manage the children during this period, she replied that she didn't want to manage them. "I want them to express themselves in the way they feel like expressing themselves."

Within one week after it was introduced, the art period was bedlam. Children were crawling under tables, climbing over tables, yelling, throwing things, and fighting. Patricia and her assistant spent most of the period trying to corral children. One day, after an exceptionally "expressive" art experience, Patricia asked, "What am I going to do?"

The next day we announced that all children who worked at their seats for five minutes of the art period would go on a special trip to the park. We repeated the rule and asked the children questions to make sure that they understood it. As the children worked, Patricia and her assistant praised the children who were working well. "You're doing a fine job. Keep it up and you'll go on the trip to the park." They did not say anything to the children who were not performing.

Four children did not go to the park. They were required to sit in their seats while we asked individual children what they were going to do at the park. "Are you going down that great big slide? Boy, is that fun!"

After the children returned from the park we asked them,

again in the presence of the four who did not go, what they had done at the park. "You really had a good time, didn't you?"

"Yeah, yeah," they agreed.

Within three days and after two more opportunities to take a park trip, Patricia could say at any time during the art period, "Okay, let's have a quiet time now. Work by yourselves," and the room would become silent. Patricia was now able to do all of the things that she had wanted to do. She could give the children a great deal of freedom to choose activities, to talk to each other, to move around the room. She had control over the children, because they were working for payoffs. At first, payoff was going to the park or having an ice-cream treat. Later, their faces showed that the real payoff came when she told them, "You're really making a nice picture."

After Patricia had been using reinforcement for several years she developed an individual style. Once she was assigned to work with a group of seven-year-old "emotionally disturbed" children who supposedly had attention spans of less than ten seconds. Because of their serious attention problems, these children had not begun formal instruction. When Patricia walked in and sat down, the children were seated in a semicircle in front of the blackboard, talking busily among themselves. Patricia didn't pay any attention to them. She didn't even look at them. Instead she wrote the numeral 4 on the board, saying "Four" rather loudly. She then smiled and made a mark on the board. One child watched her. "That's a point for me," Patricia said. "I'm really good at this game. I'm probably the smartest person you'll ever see." She then erased the 4 and wrote a 2 on the board. "Two," she said. "Oh, Patricia," she continued, "you are so smart." She gave herself another point.

By now most of the children were watching her. She wrote the numeral 7 on the board.

"Seven!" two of the children yelled.

Patricia looked at them, somewhat startled. "Nobody said you could play this game," she said.

The children laughed and nudged each other.

"You think you're smart?" Patricia asked. "Tell you what: we'll have a little race. The one who names the numeral first gets a point. I'll put my points up there and your points over here. I'm warning you, though, nobody can beat me at this game."

When the game began, all of the children responded. Every time they beat Patricia, they smiled and clapped. As soon as the children had more points than Patricia, she played the game of a poor loser. "Look at that big bug on the ceiling!" She pointed. When all the children looked up, she wrote 5 on the board and said, "Five! I won." She gave herself a point.

The children started to object, but Patricia quickly wrote 2 on the board and said, "Two," and gave herself the point. "Oh, I'm just too tricky for you. I'm way ahead. You'll never catch me now."

Within another minute the children's eyes were magnetized on Patricia. She pointed to one boy's shoes. "Why are your shoes untied?" she asked.

"Don't look! Don't look!" three or four of the children chorused. Not one of those children with the short attention spans looked.

Each ploy Patricia tried was met with the chant "Don't look! Don't look!"

Finally she wrote a numeral on the board. "Nine!" the children yelled. They were now ahead in the game. They cheered.

Patricia said, "Let's not finish the game. I'm tired and I've got a headache. And this game isn't much fun, anyhow."

"We want to play," the children said.

As the game continued, Patricia found that the children had trouble with 13. She smiled. "I know how to get you now. Every time I want a point, I'll just write 'thirteen' on the board." Patricia got exactly two points by using 13. After that, the children identified it every time.

After fifteen minutes of "drill" the children were way ahead. Grudgingly Patricia said, "Well, you won today, but you were just lucky. I'll get you next time."

"No, you won't," they said. "We'll get *you* next time."

If you had observed the children near the end of their session with Patricia, you probably wouldn't have been convinced that they were emotionally disturbed or that their attention mechanism was faulty. Patricia used simple reinforcement techniques to give them a reason for attending. She challenged them by advertising herself as being very smart, setting the children up to feel even smarter if they beat her. And when they did beat her she saw that they received a payoff for performing well, for staying on task, and for having "long attention spans."

What Causes Behavioral Change?

One important aspect of Patricia's reinforcing technique was that it capitalized on the fact that the children found it reinforcing *to do the opposite of what she said*. When she told them to look away from the chalkboard, they were reinforced for looking at the chalkboard. When she indicated that she wanted to quit, she reinforced them for continuing the game. We know from their behavior that they were reinforced for continuing. A teacher who tells children to stop doing something may actually be reinforcing them for maintaining the behavior she is trying to extinguish.

Another Becker experiment illustrates that the way to determine what is reinforcing to children is to look at their behavior. He first collected data on the number of times a teacher working with a small reading group told other children (who were at their seats), "Sit down." He then instructed the teacher to increase the number of times that she told the children to sit down. The results: when the teacher issued four times the number of "Sit downs" that she had initially, the children stood up twice as often as they did initially. When the teacher ignored the children who stood up, reduced the number of "Sit down" commands, and praised the children who were sitting and working, the number of times the children stood up dropped substantially below the number observed at the beginning of the experiment.

The teacher in the experiment was reinforcing standing-up behavior by saying, "Sit down." If children are being reinforced, they continue to engage in the activity that leads to reinforcement. Conversely, if children persist in an activity, it is reinforcing. Teachers sometimes insist that they are reinforcing children when they are actually punishing them. For example, the teacher may say that she gives the children points, but if the children show us through their behavior that they are not willing to work for points, the points are not reinforcing.

Interpreting Behavior

Another problem some teachers have is interpreting the child's behavior. Instead of seeing the child's behavior as a set of responses that have been reinforced, they see it as an expression of some inner need or drive. They fail to deal with the behavior intelligently because their interpretation gets in the way. In one experiment at the University of Chicago, preschool disadvantaged children were held and comforted every day; the curriculum was designed not to push them but to provide as much as possible for the gratification of their "needs." Compared to children in different types of programs, the children in this program had many more emotional problems. They threw far more tantrums, sucked their thumbs more, exhibited more sibling rivalry. The children in this group even had a loss of IQ during the treatment period (a rarity for preschool children in any kind of program). The program failed both as therapy and as education.

The following incident illustrates that when teachers interpret behavior in terms of the child's inner needs, they have difficulty in changing their behavior. A behaviorally oriented psychologist working in a California institution was having difficulties trying to get one of the nurses to do what was called for to change the behavior of one boy. This boy threw wild tantrums. Time and again, the psychologist told the nurse not to pay attention to the child when he threw tantrums. But every time the child threw a tantrum, the nurse picked him up and held him. The tantrums were steadily becoming more stormy and more frequent.

On many occasions the psychologist asked the nurse, "Why do you think the child throws tantrums?"

"Because he has a need to be held and loved," she answered.

"But what evidence do you have that he has a need to be held and loved?"

"He throws tantrums."

The psychologist tried to point out the weakness of the circular argument, but the nurse didn't agree with his interpretation. She insisted that she *knew* the child had needs and she *knew* what those needs were.

One day the psychologist announced to the nurse that he had discovered what was wrong with the tantrum-throwing child, and he described a rare disease. He added, "If I'm to do a proper diagnosis about whether Tommy has this disease, I'll need data. Here's what I want you to do." He explained that the nurse was to observe the exact time that the child threw each tantrum, and the nature of the tantrum, and that she was to record the data *immediately* on a chart which was in her office, over a block from the room in which she worked with Tommy.

After a few days of data collection, the nurse made the observation that there was a dramatic reduction in the child's tantrum throwing. "Very strange," she observed.

It must have seemed strange to the child too. He had been taught by the nurse that when he threw a tantrum it was always followed by the nurse picking him up and giving him a great deal of attention. Now a tantrum led to no holding and no attention from her. As soon as he threw a tantrum, she ran out of the room, leaving Tommy on the hard floor. There was still attention from the other children in the ward, who watched with interest as Tommy writhed and screamed, but it wasn't the same as being held by the nurse.

Since the other children were rewarding the tantrum behavior, the psychologist put up charts in the next room. He gave the children instructions about how they could help him (and earn points) whenever Tommy threw a tantrum. They were to go immediately to their charts in the next room and color in a strip to show when the tantrum took place.

The situation was getting grim for Tommy, whose tantrums were followed by a great exodus from the room. The nurse went one way, the other kids went another, and Tommy was all alone. Being basically intelligent, he soon figured out that there was no payoff in throwing tantrums. Within a few days he started to look for other ways to get attention and approval from the nurse. The tantrums stopped. And the nurse had learned a lesson from Tommy: Don't be blinded by how you feel. If children persist in particular behaviors, they are being rewarded for those behaviors. If you want the behavior to stop, withdraw the reward and start rewarding the kind of behavior you want strengthened.

A number of behavioral psychologists have noted that many teachers are functionally blind to what goes on in the classroom. Not only do they fail to give an accurate account of how a particular child acted; they are almost unable to tell what happened immediately before the incident. The psychologists have noted further that if these teachers record events in the way the nurse did, they can then start to attend to the conditions they had not observed. The act of recording somehow allows a teacher (or a nurse or a psychologist) to focus on observations and reduce the noise that is associated with each observation. Some behaviorists train their people by having them record frequency of behaviors and the events that antecede the behavior. Within a short period of time, these teachers know more about behavioral principles than students who have learned all of the jargon in two years of graduate school.

Punishment as a Powerful Tool

We have talked about positive rewards and paying off children for exhibiting appropriate behavior. But punishment is a more explosive subject. Physical punishment is considered an unenlightened practice, particularly by people who are never placed in a position of dealing with children who cannot be reached through positive reinforcement. But there are occasions when punishment can make the difference between teaching a child now and perhaps wasting months while he "comes around." In the meantime, the child may be depriving others of their chance to be taught, injuring himself or others, and demanding an incredible amount of attention. Punishment is a tool as effective for a teacher as a DPT shot is for an M.D. And like a DPT shot, punishment should not be overused or misused.

We can illustrate a punishment solution with Sherry, a four-year-old girl who couldn't talk. If you showed Sherry a picture of a farm scene she could find the cow, the fence, the grass, and the clouds. When she attempted to deal with more abstract concepts, however, she became confused because she couldn't keep the words straight and as a result couldn't follow the chain of reasoning. Sherry was on the verge of severe social maladjustment. In a year she would be going to school, but she did not have the verbal equipment necessary to engage in many activities with her peers. She was headed for relative isolation or for playing the role of puppy dog with her peers.

Sherry was in a special program at the Hearing and Speech Center in Eugene, Oregon. She worked for one and a half hours every afternoon in a small group with other children who had language problems. Her teacher was very competent in using positive rewards. However, no reward was strong enough to entice Sherry to talk. For Sherry to master a new sound, she would need hundreds and hundreds of trials. She cooperated on only a few.

Let's look in on a session a week after the sound *rrr* was introduced. The teacher writes the letter *r* on the board. "Everybody, what sound is this?"

"Rrr," the other children in the group say.

"Mnyoo," Sherry said.

"Emil and Margo and Sandy, good job," the teacher says. "Good saying *rrr*. Let's do it again. When I touch the sound, you say it. Keep on saying it as long as I touch it."

She touches the sound.

"Rrrr."

"Mnyoo."

"Rrrrrrr," the teacher says, looking at Sherry. "Say that. *Rrrrr*."

Sherry looks away.

"Come on, Sherry, you can do it. Remember, if you work hard, you're going to get your treat. Come on, *rrrrrrr*."

Sherry looks down.

The teacher has worked with Sherry for three weeks and has never used any punishment. She has had some success with rewarding Sherry. But attempting to say things is obviously punishing for Sherry, and the rewards haven't been enough to entice responses.

Teacher: "Sherry, say *rrrrr*."

No response.

Teacher: "Sherry, stand up."

No response.

Teacher stands Sherry up rather vigorously. "Sherry, sit down."

Sherry slumps back into the chair and starts to cry.

"You've got to try, Sherry. Stand up."

No response. Again the teacher stands her up.

"Sit down."

No response. The teacher pushes her into the chair.

Sherry, who is crying loudly, squirms to get out of the chair.

"Sit down!" the teacher says and pushes her back into the chair.

"Sherry, stand up," the teacher says.

Sherry stands up.

"Good," the teacher says. "Sit down."

Sherry sits down.

"Good," the teacher says. "Stand up."

Sherry stands up.

"Sit down."

Sherry sits down.

"Now say *rrrr*. Come on, you can do it."

Sherry looks to the side and says, "Mnyoo."

"Good, you're trying now. Just keep it up. Look at me."

Sherry looks.

"*Rrrrrr*. Say it with me, *rrrrr*."

"Nnnnllllloo," Sherry says.

"You're going to get it, Sherry. You're really trying now."

The scene was certainly not a pleasant one. Shy little Sherry is the kind of girl you'd like to hold and protect. Yet there are times when a little hurt now is indeed little compared with the constant, gnawing pain that the child will experience later.

The punishment sessions had to be repeated several times. After the third session Sherry had apparently learned that it was more punishing not to talk than it was to talk. From that time on, the teacher never had to use punishment again. Sherry tried and the teacher rewarded her attempts.

"You've almost got it, Sherry. Good trying. Let's do it again."

"Uuuuuurrrrrr."

Within a few days after the last punishment session, Sherry's mother made the observation that Sherry practiced saying things when she was alone in her room. Sherry's mother also reported that Sherry vocalized a lot more at mealtimes and that she seemed much happier than she'd ever been.

Within five months, Sherry progressed from a nontalker, who couldn't say one word, to a girl who could say several hundred simple statements, which she used constantly. And she was very close to mastering many more. At the end of the five-month period, Sherry had gained seventeen IQ points. She had progressed beyond the average child her age in basic prereading and arithmetic skills.

Consider the punishment that the teacher provided in the realistic context of Sherry's life. Since Sherry found trying to talk very difficult and punishing, she would have resisted trying to talk until she encountered those inevitable social situations when she would be ridiculed by other kids and thereby punished for trying to talk. At this point, Sherry would have had to find some other form of escape from the situation.

Sherry's teacher used punishment minimally and saw to it that Sherry would be reinforced *for trying to talk*. She could have used less effective and more palatable techniques, but she chose a course that would produce results now, while Sherry was only four years old, rather than when she was six or eleven.

"Selling" Privileges

We have noted that operant techniques are effective with severely handicapped children. They are equally effective with a classroom of "normal" children, who generally require less payoff to prime them. They are quite willing to work for something that the teacher treats as important; if the teacher demonstrates to the children that performing well in arithmetic is important, the children will respond.

A teacher on the West Coast was working with a group of first-grade children who were labeled immature. She "sold" the children everything from free time to drawing paper. By January they had progressed farther in their academics than a group of "mature" children would be expected to progress. The teacher had one problem, which was that the children were constantly asking to go to the bathroom. One day the teacher announced a rule change (children are *never* upset by rule changes if a teacher handles the change in a matter-of-fact way). "From now on, you can go to the bathroom as many times as you wish, but if you go at any time except the recess break and the lunch break, the trip costs fifteen points." She reviewed the rule to make sure that the children understood it. In the classroom a period at the easel cost only eight points; five minutes of extra recess cost ten points; a period in the record booths cost only twelve points. A trip to the bathroom was therefore expensive. Virtually no children asked to go to the bathroom after the change in rules. The teacher didn't tell the children that they couldn't go. She simply arranged the contingencies so that it became a question of *how much they wanted to take a bathroom trip*. Through the use of points she had manipulated the children, but she did so in a way that *they* made the decision about their activities.

What Is Adjustment?

The operant philosophy suggests that you don't have to wait for a child to become well adjusted before working with him.

Psychological adjustment is one of the more frequent goals expressed by the traditional educator. Curiously, the traditional educator isn't prepared to create appropriate adjustment—he's merely prepared to talk about it. Further, he believes that adjustment is part of the child's makeup or personality.

Studies on children's behavior suggest that the child's adjustment is far more specific than the traditionalists indicate. Psychological adjustment is related to specific activities. Nobody is "well adjusted" to every situation. The person who is confident in quite a few situations may feel totally inept and frustrated in such situations as cooking dinner for fifty, repairing the washing machine, taking a group of three-year-olds to the park, lecturing on functions to a group of mathematicians, or entertaining three Chinese chicken raisers who can't speak English. "Adjustment" is not an entity in itself. One must be adjusted in *doing something*. The behaviors that children exhibit are usually appropriate in some situations. Aggressive behavior is perfectly appropriate when the child is playing football or some other contact sport. Talking about adjustment in the abstract doesn't usually tell the teacher what the child has been taught, nor does it imply what she should do to change the behavior. It is far more productive to look at the kind of adjustment we want the child to make—in which situations, and by exhibiting specific kinds of behaviors. With this specification, the teacher can focus on the child's behavior and use techniques that will change the behavior. Once it has been changed, she will have erased all clues that the child has "problems."

We have worked with children who had been judged emotionally incapable of performing in a classroom situation. One such child was Danny. At home Danny cried, lied, threw tantrums, and engaged in a full range of maladaptive behavior. His behavior, however, was very well adapted to the way his parents treated him. When he came to school he exhibited these same behaviors. Within four months he had been taught that different behaviors are reinforced in school. Danny's school behavior was now quite acceptable. Danny's home behavior didn't change, however. He had discovered that his old behaviors were still appropriate at home, and he continued to use them. A psychologist who had observed Danny at home was more than surprised to observe him in school. "I just can't believe it," he said. Apparently what he couldn't believe was that Danny was intelligent enough to adjust to two obviously different situations. Nearly everybody learns to use a different set of words when talking to his peers and to a minister. He learns to "play roles," each keyed to specific situations.

The Null Solution to Adjustment Problems

To succeed with the Dannys as well as with more normal children, the schools must identify the situations to which they want the children to adjust.

If we want them to adjust to situations in which they are being taught new academic skills, we must recognize that new learning is relatively punishing for naïve children. When the child learns new things, he must concentrate; he must abandon old responses and experiment with new ones. Although this method may seem sensible, there is a strong tendency among traditional educators to search for a solution that will "avoid" the problems in a new learning situation. One such solution is the open classroom. Silberman's book *Crisis in the Classroom* presents the argument that the American classroom is a joyless place and concludes that the form of the classroom must be modified so that children choose the activities they wish to pursue. If a child wants to hammer a block for three days, he is allowed to do so. The belief is that when he has saturated his need to hammer, he will do something else; soon he will choose to learn to read.

Techniques to "Motivate" Adjustment

The Silberman solution implies that there is no way to make children "motivated" or well adjusted in a structured learning situation. It assumes that the only reasonable solution is not to try to force these activities on the children, but, rather, to find activities that are reinforcing for the child, regardless of how fruitless these activities may be. The inevitable harvest of this philosophy is lots of children who never master basic skills. Just as certain, those who advocated this philosophy will blame the children, saying, in effect, "That child wasn't meant to read. The reason he didn't choose reading was that he wasn't ready."

Granted, the classroom is a joyless place. Granted it is ineffective in teaching children. However, we can put joy back into the classroom without ignoring the professional responsibility with which the schools are charged. By using reinforcement techniques, we can structure situations so that children actually enjoy learning to read. We once did a simple demonstration with five-year-olds. We gave them a choice between a treat, followed by a recess, and learning a new arithmetic operation that the teacher said was "too hard for you to master." Six of seven children chose to learn the operation, and mastered it after twenty minutes of instruction. They all reacted with smiles and apparent pride when the teacher expressed surprise about such young kids being able to learn such a difficult operation.

In another example, a student teacher was working successfully with a group of incorrigible eight-year-olds. The teacher, a skilled young man, had worked out a format that was quite successful. Before presenting a new task, he would place one or two M & M's on a small table that was next to him. He would then announce in the tradition of a good carnival barker, "All right. This next task is worth two M & M's." He would then present a question to each child. If the child didn't respond correctly, he would say, "My turn." He would ask himself the question, give the correct answer, award himself two M & M's, and eat them with a great show of enjoyment.

The problem with the procedure was that after three weeks of working with the group the teacher had gained fifteen pounds. I told him to drop the M & M's. "Oh, no," he said. "I remember how they were before I introduced the M & M's. I don't want to go through that again—kicking, fighting."

I told him that I would work with the group and show him that they weren't hooked on the M & M's. I cut up a number of squares of yellow paper and showed them to the kids. "Do you see what this is? Yellow paper. And you're going to have a choice on every task I present. You can choose the M & M's, or you can choose the yellow paper. I know that you're young kids and you'll choose that kid stuff—the M & M's. I'm choosing the yellow paper. The first task is worth one piece of yellow paper or four M & M's." I presented the task, and before asking the first child which he would choose I said to one of the other kids, "I'll bet he chooses the kid stuff. Little kids like candy." All but one child chose yellow paper. That kid was about to pop the M & M's into his mouth when one of the children next to him said, "Kid stuff." The child looked up and saw that the others in the group were watching with disgusted expressions. He shrugged. "I was just going to put it in my pocket and eat it later," he said.

For the rest of the period, all the children chose yellow paper. They were quite proud of their yellow papers when the period was completed. "Look how smart I am; I got *seven* yellow papers." "That's nothin'. I got *eight*."

The M & M's had served a purpose when the teacher first worked with the children. Since then, they had learned that instruction can be fun. They were now hooked on the activity. The M & M's merely functioned as a certificate, a symbol of their achievement, and an indication of the teacher's approval.

The traditionalist may argue that it is frightening to think that there is a technology capable of making children respond to pieces of yellow paper as if they were status symbols. Actually, it is encouraging to think that the technology has the potential to change children's behavior so that they respond to the challenge, the symbols, the achievement characteristic of the highly motivated student. It is possible to misuse this technology, but, as Skinner pointed out in *The Technology of Teaching*, "It could maximize the genetic endowment of each student; it could make him as skillful, competent, and informed as possible; it could build the greatest diversity of interests."

The teacher will either apply this technology or she won't. If she doesn't, she will probably do unwitting harm by changing children in undesirable ways, by making the classroom a joyless place, and by failing to bring around the children who don't come into the classroom already equipped with the behaviors that are needed to perform well in school.

5

Preparing the Teacher

The Traditional Curriculum

We have seen that the examples the teacher presents cause children to perform in predictable ways and that the manner in which a teacher reacts to children causes the differences in their performance. It would seem to follow, therefore, that teachers should receive careful instruction in how to behave—how to construct demonstrations that teach, and how to reinforce. If we were to train surgeons the way we train teachers, we would give the student several general courses in anatomy (with emphasis on reference books that give the "specific details"), several courses on the social foundations, the history and the philosophy of medicine, and a survey of medical practices (none of which are current within the last eight years). Then the practitioner-to-be would spend eight weeks as an assistant in a butcher shop, after which he would receive certification.

The traditional teacher training program provided in ninety percent of the universities and colleges apparently doesn't recognize that after certification the teacher will sit down with a group of children and present examples and say things; that she will react to the responses of the children, correcting their mistakes and making sure that they are turned on. The teacher's training unfortunately does not start with the assumption that a teacher's behavior is the central feature of the teaching situation.

Mary's Conditioning Begins

We can illustrate this by looking at Mary, a typical product of an average traditional college of education. Mary went through a basic four-year course provided by a state college of education; she also had one year of graduate training, for which she received a master's degree. Mary probably couldn't summarize what she had learned from her training, because the emphasis was placed on vague issues. What she learned was strong emotional reactions to words. *Process, creativity, discovery, democracy, decision-making, open, experience, guidance,* and *rapport* all produced a positive, reassuring feeling in Mary. On the other hand, such words as *control, dictate, manipulate, product, discipline, rote,* and *drill* produced a negative feeling, an ill-formed uneasiness.

Mary's feelings about the words did not evolve from an intellectual understanding of instruction and its problems. The feelings came about through a well-designed program in which Mary was punished for thinking or questioning. Mary was simply shown, through hundreds of demonstrations, that when a "good" word was said, a certain type of reaction was called for. Any other reaction was met with scorn and the tacit threat that such inappropriate behavior would lead to a poor grade.

Most teachers have been conditioned in the same way Mary was. You get a rough indication of the success of the program by asking a small group of teachers to describe a "creative child." We presented this task to a number of groups of traditional teachers. The results are remarkably similar in every case. Teachers will list as characteristics of the creative child every "positive" characteristic they have learned. They will indicate that the creative child cooperates with others, respects the opinions of others, has a wide range of interests, and loves to learn.

In addition to a strong feeling about certain words, Mary learned one basic principle from her college instruction: teachers differ in their approach to children, just as children differ in their approach to learning. This position assumes that there isn't much that we can do about changing a teacher's behavior except perhaps to change her personality.

Mary studied her first education course, an introduction to educational principles, carefully. The textbook was *Education for the Open Society*, by Aubrey Haan (published by Allyn and Bacon). On page 28, Mary underlined a passage under the heading "Schools: Their Purpose":

> The first principle of true teaching is that nothing can be taught. The teacher is not an instructor or taskmaster, he is a helper and a guide. His business is to suggest and not to impose. He does not actually train the pupil's mind, he only shows him how to perfect his instruments of knowledge, and helps and encourages him in the process. He does not impart knowledge to him, he shows him how to acquire knowledge for himself. He does not call forth the knowledge that is within; he only shows him where it lies and how it can be habituated to rise to the surface. The distinction that reserves this principle for the teaching of adolescent and adult minds and denies its application to the child, is a conservative and unintelligent doctrine.

Mary took this passage seriously. She didn't know that the position expressed is basically irresponsible and sets the stage for wholesale educational malpractice.

During her first year in education, Mary questioned statements that she read. The problem was that Mary had no basis for asking *intelligent* questions. She knew nothing about teaching and only a little more about kids. She marked a passage in her textbook that dealt with the omniscient concept of reading readiness:

> . . . Readiness for reading is by no means a mechanical condition made up of left-to-right eye movements, eye focus, and vocabulary development alone. Readiness to read also represents an emotional readiness. This readiness may consist of willingness to grow up, to grow out of the five-year-old stage and into latency and, in another sense, to give up the Oedipal conflict. Children who read phenomenally early may reflect, however, not exceptional intelligence, though this may be present, but a deprivation of contact with the real—the mother, for example. Reading here becomes a substitute for felt love. Extremely early reading should be studied closely for the possibility of pathology that may cause difficulty in other areas of the child's life.

Mary didn't understand that the description of readiness doesn't imply any action that the teacher can take.

In another chapter of *Education for the Open Society,* the author analyzed the dynamics of learning arithmetic:

> The relationships of child and parent, as well as those among siblings, may also be involved in learning. Among siblings, the desire to be different may urge one child to accept mathematics as important, and another to reject it on that account. Sibling rivalry may produce overachievement as a result of a child's desire to be loved more than his competing sibling. . . . Maternally overprotected children tend to do poorly at mathematics, but well in reading. On the other hand, some studies have indicated that when children are unable to break their strong ties with their mother, difficulty in mathematics may occur. Or to say it another way,

the child cannot free himself for symbolic manipulation because the first and primary person has remained so real and actual that the most important symbolic removal cannot occur without conflict.

Mary's reaction was a mixture of confusion and curiosity. She wasn't sure what the author was trying to say.

Page 244 of Mary's textbook gives some hints about the type of frustration she experienced in her first course:

> The elementary social studies teacher cannot be thought of as purveyor of bits of content over which he has managed to exercise some command.
>
> *How to prepare the teacher for this broader pre-service and an in-service problem.* It is going to take time for teachers to acquire the professional sophistication needed to work with children in the ways suggested in this book. Certainly, their knowledge of dynamic psychology needs to be increased, as does their command of such anthropological conceptualizations as socialization.

Next to the sentence that refers to the professional sophistication needed to work with children in the ways suggested by the author, Mary had written, "What ways?" Mary hadn't yet been conditioned not to question about specifics. She was still able to see that while the author indicated a need for training, he was incapable of specifying the nature of that training. By the end of the year, Mary had already developed some conditioned responses to good words and bad words. In the back of her mind she knew that the statements and "principles" she was learning about education related to the activity that she recognized as "teaching." The descriptions of readiness, of discovery learning, of teaching social science, of diagnosing children, all were phrased so that Mary wasn't quite sure how they related to that activity in which the teacher stands in front of the children. She concluded that there must be a connection because the authorities indicate that there is one.

Mary's Exposure to Teaching Techniques

Mary took three education courses during the first semester of her junior year. The only course in reading that she was to take as an undergraduate was a three-hour course that met twice a week. It covered not only reading instructions for the beginner, but reading practices through the sixth grade. The textbook for the course was *Effective Teaching of Reading,* by Harris, and it endorsed the look-say method and the language-experience approach (*à la* Sylvia Ashton Warner). Mary didn't know that quite a few comparative studies have demonstrated that these are the worst two approaches in terms of the performance of the children.

The textbook discussion of beginning reading gave Mary very little specific information about what to do. Perhaps the most specific element in the chapter—"Beginning to Read"— was an actual reprinted page from a typical look-say pre-primer. About three pages of text dealt with "instructional procedures."

In the conclusion of the section, Harris noted that the student teacher should make a careful study of lesson plans and go through the material step by step, to make "the procedures that have been described in the preceding few pages . . . vividly meaningful." Mary's class did not have time for such explorations, and the descriptions didn't become vividly meaningful to her.

In the next paragraph Harris indicates that the instructions provided by manuals are crutches for inexperienced teachers and that the experienced teacher becomes selective, using the manual as a source of suggestions rather than a set of directions. Unfortunately, Harris didn't specify a reasonable basis for selecting and rejecting. The implication is that it is a matter of personal preference or taste.

In effect, Harris was saying, "I'm not giving you detailed information about the method; I'm not indicating what constitutes experience and what criteria you will later use to decide how to choose activities from different basals; but when you're experienced, you won't have to follow the method that I haven't described."

Harris followed the discussion of look-say basals with a section headed "Alternative Methods," in which phonic methods are discussed. The discussion is about one page long, and nearly half of it is an appeal which begins with the telling sentence, "Cautious educators are aware, however, that an outstanding new discovery in science is not accepted until it has been verified by independent investigators."

Although a great deal of research supports the conclusion that the more structured phonic programs produce better readers, Mary's class was not told about this research. They were left with the one-page discussion of phonics as an "alternative method." Seven students in Mary's class later taught first grade. It comes as no surprise that only one of them is a good reading teacher (judged by the performance of the children she teaches).

Mary underlined each of the few specific suggestions provided by Harris. On page 41 are three concrete suggestions about managing problem children. The first is that the mothers of timid children should be allowed to remain in the classroom if a beginning child is upset. The idea is to "make the weaning process a gradual one."

The second suggestion is that rebellious or stubborn children should be removed from the group and provided with quiet individual activities. The third suggestion is that if this behavior continues beyond the first couple of months, the teacher should discuss the problem with the parents, in the hope that they can provide some corrective measures. If that fails, the teacher should consult the principal, guidance counselor, or psychologist, since the problem may require the kind of treatment "that no teacher can provide."

Mary was in no position to evaluate the effectiveness of the suggestions, since her college had not yet afforded her the opportunity to work with kids. Ironically, she later tried each of the three techniques and found that none worked.

At the time, Mary was teaching first grade. She used the long weaning period prescribed by Harris and noted that the children performed worse when their parents were present. It wasn't until the next year that the first-grade teacher in the next room (who had virtually no behavior problems) told Mary, "The kids have learned to be ingrown around their parents. As long as the parent is in the classroom, the kid's going to act goofy. You must get the parents out of the classroom *immediately*. In fact, don't let them into the classroom on the first day of school." Mary tried this teacher's technique, and it worked much better than Harris' technique.

Mary followed Harris' advice of removing stubborn children from the group and giving them quiet individual activities. These children didn't seem to come around. If anything, they tended to become even more stubborn as the year progressed. Mary never learned that removing children in this manner and providing them with another activity may be just what the children want. The procedure teaches them a simple formula for getting out of a boring group activity: put on the stubborn act. It invariably leads to removal from the group, teacher attention, and individual activity that is often more fun than group activity, and it may be followed by a nice warm lecture/pep talk from the teacher.

Mary also found that the third technique, that of telling parents, principals, psychologists, and counselors about behavior problems, didn't work very well, either. In some cases the parents beat the children, but too often the beatings didn't help. When she referred the children to the psychologist it was sometimes months before he saw them, and then she often got a written report that described the child's problems with no indication of what Mary should do to correct them. In Mary's district, over two hundred children were referred to the psychologist at the beginning of each year, and fewer than half of them had been seen by the year's end.

During Mary's junior year, she also took a methods course in which she made up lesson plans. Although the professor said her scrapbook was one of the most interesting he had seen, Mary didn't feel that she really learned anything about "methods" for working with children.

Real-Life Experiences

In her senior year, Mary student-taught for eight weeks, a sobering experience for her. The third-grade teacher under whom Mary studied was, in Mary's opinion, lazy. During the first several weeks of Mary's student teaching, the teacher gave Mary various odd tasks that the teacher didn't want to do, such as grading the children's papers. The teacher let Mary take over the classroom for an hour every day while the teacher went to the teachers' lounge for a long smoke. As soon as the teacher left, the children started to act up. When she returned they scrambled for their seats. Later Mary told the teacher, "I seem to have trouble controlling them. But you don't have any problem at all. How do you do it?"

"It's just experience," she replied.

Mary later realized that this kind of reply is fashionable and implies "I'm just a natural teacher."

Mary was disappointed in the student-teaching report she received from her supervising teacher. In part it said, "Intelligent, hard working, but not able to relate well to children." Mary had discovered that working with children was not as natural as she had supposed it would be.

Later that spring Mary graduated and became a licensed teacher, having completed her foundation courses in the history and philosophy and methods of education. She had satisfied the requirement for student teaching. Her grades were mostly A's.

The irony of Mary's education is that it violated every objective that traditional education has for children. Mary didn't learn by doing. She was not afforded any concrete experiences with children until her senior year. Since she was very carefully shielded from encountering children, she had no basis for exploring. Mary was the victim of propaganda, serious omissions, emotional arguments that preempt scientific questions, and "theories" that had nothing to do with instruction. She was told that John Dewey was some form of deity while those who opposed the traditional line were unenlightened conservatives. Her instruction provided her with no concrete basis for evaluating B. F. Skinner, John Dewey, or any other educational philosopher.

After graduating, Mary taught first grade in a middle-class suburban school. She found the experience frustrating. As she gained "experience," her trouble managing children didn't lessen. She remembered a sentence from Harris' book on reading: "Perhaps the old adage, 'if at first you don't succeed, try, try again,' should be interpreted as meaning, 'try another method.'" Mary didn't know that Harris' rule of thumb was a beautiful rule for operating so that you'll probably never find out what works and what doesn't. Mary did many different things; when something seemed to work, however, she was never sure which of the many things she had done accounted for the change in the child's behavior.

Learning the Theory of Failure

After teaching for two years Mary returned to the college to work on her master's degree. During her first semester of graduate school, her philosophy of education seemed to crystallize. The final step in Mary's conditioning took place in a course in remedial and corrective reading. The professor, Dr. Larson, was considered a leading authority on reading and had what Mary thought was a very practical approach to teaching. He was neither maudlin nor insensitive. He identified many of the problems that Mary had faced, even if he didn't give ready solutions. But he showed that he *cared!*

Zintz, the author of the textbook for the course, *Corrective Reading*, seemed to be aware of critical problems in teaching problem children:

> The range of differences in a given class will increase through the year and from year to year as the class progresses through school. If the range of reading ability in second grade is four years on standardized reading tests, it is to be expected that, with good teaching, by the eighth grade this range will be about ten years. Teachers who feel a strong compulsion to work especially hard with the slowest group in the class, hoping to get them to achieve at grade level, are not only attempting the impossible, but may be neglecting the other groups who have greater capacity.

Mary didn't know that the "impossible" could be achieved if the teacher knew something about teaching. To her, Zintz's proclamation seemed reasonable and consistent with her experience. Later, when she was to violate Zintz's principle (as she did when she worked extra hard with little Jimmy), her reward would be frustration.

In another chapter Mary read:

> One of the serious problems in school is that of allowing children to "sit through" weeks and weeks of school attendance without developmental learning taking place. Classroom teachers need to be more accepting of, and much less defensive about, this fact. When adequately accepting and less defensive, they will ask for and demand outside help for problems which are not amenable to the limited individual instruction they

can provide. Such children, for whom the school is not offering successful instruction, might be excluded from the school. At least in this way their problem will not be "unrecognized," and once it is made clear that the child needs special help most communities can provide it.

Terry is a case in point. Terry was referred to the educational clinic in the spring of his eighth-grade year. His parents had been notified by the principal that the school would be glad to give him an eighth-grade diploma if the parents would promise not to enroll him in the ninth grade in high school. With this "threat" the parents could no longer remain complacent as they had up to this time. They took the problem to their minister who made inquiries and found a reading clinic for a diagnostic examination for the boy. The fact that special arrangements were made and the boy learned in fifteen months of tutoring to read well at the sixth-grade level indicates that the school would have done a big favor both to the boy and to his parents if they had excluded him five years earlier when he enrolled in fifth grade as a non-reader. As it was, the school allowed him to sit through one year each in fifth and sixth grades and two years each in seventh and eighth grades as a non-reader, and then asked that he not come back! Many referrals to reading clinics come from ministers, school nurses, and social workers instead of from classroom teachers themselves who should be calling for help with difficult problems.

One of the diagrams presented in Zintz's book struck Mary as a culmination of all that she had learned about learning and children. The diagram showed the interaction of all the variables upon which learning depends.

Mary understood only too well that a child's learning is delicately balanced between many sometimes mysterious factors. How is a teacher to know whether a child has had a lack of

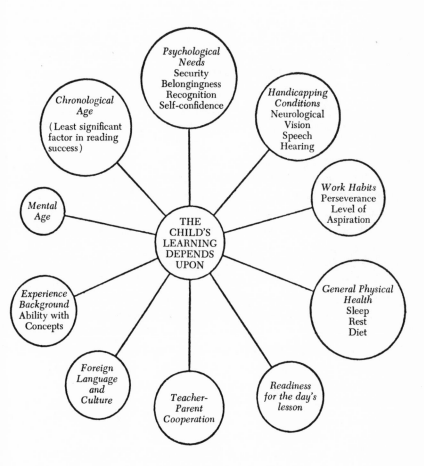

A Child's Learning Depends on Many Factors

sleep? How is she to know what kinds of emotional problems he is having? Zintz seemed to do a commendable job of putting the various factors into a diagram. Mary failed to notice that the teacher's behavior is not included in the diagram; nor is the nature of the instructional material. These are *the only two factors that are under the teacher's control;* yet they are conspicuously absent. Another subtle point that Mary failed to grasp was that the Zintz diagram is arranged so that the responsibility for learning rests with the child. If he succeeds, we marvel over the wondrous mystery of learning. If he fails we cannot blame the instruction, because the diagram doesn't seriously admit to the possibility that instruction determines whether or not children learn.

As a graduate student Mary was far more credulous than she had been as a sophomore. She didn't even question this statement by Zintz: "For the child who has difficulty, the teacher will be able to judge when to interject questions, stop to discuss, and generally lend encouragement." Could this astute instructionalist and diagnostician be the same teacher who let Terry sit in school for *years* without teaching him how to read?

Mary was fully conditioned. She had come to believe in the words that had bombarded her since she first entered elementary education. In the process she had become something of a fatalist. A teacher's job, she felt, is to be there when a child is ready. When he is ready, he will learn in his own style. If a child fails, there must be something wrong with his past, his nervous system, or his environment. Or perhaps he will be a late bloomer.

Mary believed in words because she had nothing else for support. As teacher, she didn't wear a badge or a uniform; words were the only symbol of her profession.

The Products of Traditional Teacher Training

Mary's training is similar to that offered at most state teachers' colleges or colleges of education. The regimen is fairly well outlined by tradition. Teachers who plan to work in the primary grades may study only one three-hour course in reading, usually designed for first- through sixth-grade teachers. The students may meet as infrequently as once a week for twelve weeks. Quite frequently students in elementary education must spend more time learning about physical education and recreation than learning about teaching reading.

Students may be required to take only one course in arithmetic (sometimes presented by the mathematics department) and one course in social sciences. The rest of their course work is devoted to the introduction to education, social foundations, general methods of education, art in the elementary school, children's literature, and student teaching. Sometimes the curriculum calls for a course in human development and learning which is a survey in labeling and misinformation about children.

The undergraduate course is sad, but not as sad as the graduate course. School systems often require teachers to take refresher courses in colleges. Many school-district pay scales favor teachers who have master's degrees. The college is in trouble if it flunks teachers, but the teachers too often come back with their learning abilities corroded from inactivity. The result is that graduate-level education courses are often *more sophomoric versions of the courses presented on the undergraduate level*. A professor at the University of Illinois explained the logic of this practice to me. "If we don't lower the standards for them," he said, "they will go to some inferior institution like Northern Illinois to get their degree." I was unable to follow the argument.

The tragic policy in master's programs is usually to pass the teachers, whether or not they understand the base-eight number system or even how to count on their fingers in base ten. As a professor of mathematics explained to me, "There is no way that some of them could ever pass a course that had any standards, but you can't flunk them. Your flunk may mean that they don't get their degree. They don't want to take the course. Most of them won't teach math anyhow. And I'm not going to keep them from getting their degree. I had to make some of them promise that they would never ever teach math if I passed them. They promised—and I passed them."

A Different Approach

Mary is the product of her education. She reflects the lack of concern with specifics and details. She is a sloppy teacher because she has never even seen good teaching. Not so with Linda, who is the product of a different kind of education.

Linda works with high-risk kindergarten children in a school about three miles from Mary's school. For the last two years, she has succeeded in teaching every child to read reasonably well by the end of the year. Some read quite a bit better than the others. Even children who are like Andy have taken their first steps in decoding and read better than he will by the time he completes the fifth grade.

Before we examine Linda's training, let's watch her work with the children. She is seated near the corner of a room on a low chair in front of six children. In her hand is a book with the tasks that she will present. To her right is the chalkboard.

"Everybody, stand up. . . . Sit down. . . . Stand up. . . . Good. Now stand up." One boy sits down, smiles, and stands up again. "We fooled somebody," Linda says. "Let's try it again. You've got to listen. Sit down. . . . Close your eyes. Open your eyes. . . . Stand up. . . . Stand up. . . . Sit down. . . . Sit down. . . . Close your eyes." Linda opens the presentation book and holds it up. "Okay, open your eyes."

As soon as the children open their eyes, she says, "Remember the rules. I'll go as fast as you can go. When you can name all the sounds on this page without making a mistake, I'll turn the page."

She holds her finger a few inches from the letter *n* on the page. "When I touch it, you say it." She touches it.

"Nnnnnn," the children say as long as she touches the sound.

"Good," Linda says and moves to the next sound and then the next and the next.

On the sound ĕ as in *end*, some of the children call it *iiiii*, as in *it*.

Quickly, Linda writes both sounds on the board. She points to the *i*. "Some of you told me about this sound, but I asked you about *this* sound." She touches the *e*. "Everybody, what sound is this?"

The children say, "Ĕĕĕĕĕ."

Now Linda touches the *i*. The children respond somewhat weakly.

"Iiiiii," Linda helps them. "Again, what sound is this? . . ."

Linda goes from the *i* to the *e* and back to the *i* until all of the children are firm. Then she says, "You've got it now."

The children smile. One girl says, "I smart."

"You sure are," Linda says. "Let's go back to the beginning of the page and start over." She points to the *e*. "Remember what you're going to say when we get to this sound. What are you going to say?"

"Ĕĕĕĕĕ."

This time, as Linda points they respond correctly, and they complete the page without a mistake.

"Good job," Linda says. "Let's see how fast we can do the next page."

Quickly, she turns to a page that displays a series of short words: *are, far, mar, bar*. Linda points to *are*. "This is one of those hard words. Look it over and get ready to tell me the word." She pauses about two seconds. She points to the word, says, "Everybody," and touches under the word.

"Are," the children respond.

"Good remembering," Linda says. "Get ready to say the sounds in *are*." As Linda points to the letters, the children say, "Aaa" (as in *at*) and "rrrr," without pausing between sounds.

"But we don't say *aaar*. What do we say?"

"Are," the children respond.

"Good. This word is *are*." Then Linda touches the first letter in *far*. "Rhymes with *are* . . ."

Children: "Far."

Linda points to the first letter in *mar*. "And this must be . . ."

"Mar."

Linda touches the respective words as she says, "Are, *fff*ar, *mmmm*mar." Now she touches *bar*. "So this must be . . ."

"Bar."

As Linda points to different words on the page, the group identifies each. Then she calls on three different children to read words. Next she passes out a "take-home" to each child. A take-home is a short story on newsprint. "Everybody, point under the first word and get ready to read." She looks to make sure that every child is pointing. "Get ready . . ." Linda claps.

"A," the children say.

"Next word . . ." Again Linda looks to make sure that all the children are pointing under the appropriate word. "Get ready . . ." She claps.

"Fat," the children say.

"Next word . . ." Linda claps for each word.

The children read, ". . . cat . . . went . . . to . . . the . . ." Some of them have trouble with the word *park*.

Linda quickly writes the word on the board. She covers up the *p* and the *k*. "Everybody, what word?"

"Are."

Linda says, "If this is *are*—" she uncovers the *p*—"this must be . . ."

"Par," the children say.

Linda says, "If this is *par*—" she uncovers the *k*—"this must be . . ."

"Park," the children say.

"Remember that word," Linda says. "We'll come back to it. Okay, everybody touch the first word in the story and get ready to read. We're going to move a little faster this time, so you have to think. Get ready, get ready." Clap . . . clap . . . clap.

The children read, "A . . . fat . . . cat . . . went . . . to . . . the . . . park."

"Good remembering *park*. Everybody, where did the fat cat go?"

"To the park."

"Who went to the park?"

Some children respond weakly.

"Let's read the sentence again," Linda says. "And see who went to the park. Fingers under the first word. Get ready . . ." After the children read through the word *went*, Linda says, "Everybody, who went to the park?"

"A fat cat," the children respond.

"Is that right?" Linda asks. "Show me where it tells you that a fat cat went to the park. I think a skinny rabbit went to the park."

The children giggle and say, "No, no, that's silly." Then they point to the words *a fat cat*.

Different Product: Different Training

Linda's training was quite different from Mary's, which didn't have any strong commitment to the idea that the teacher could be taught effective teaching behaviors. It assumed that the children who were destined to learn would learn and that those destined to fail would fail. The basic premise of Linda's training was that teachers, like kids, are capable of mastering skills if these skills are carefully taught. The focus of Linda's training was on the *detailed* techniques that a teacher must have in order to work effectively with *all* children, not merely those who have already been taught much of what the teacher is assigned to teach.

Linda's training took place over two years at a state university. The program was "experimental," in that the state agreed to waive some of the mandated requirements for teacher training. The state agreed to treat the products of this experimental program on an equal basis with the students who came from the tried-and-true training programs such as the one Mary went through.

Linda began teaching children on the sixth day of her training. The first five days were designed to prepare her for the classroom work.

On the first day, Linda and twenty-five other neophytes met in a large classroom. A young woman who introduced herself as Doris, and who was not much older than Linda, outlined the program. "During the year, you will work every morning from nine to twelve in the classroom, teaching first-graders. You will be responsible for the performance of your children. You will have a supervisor who will monitor your performance. Your supervisor will observe you at least twice a week and give you specific assignments that you are responsible for carrying out. In addition to the work in the classroom, you will take courses in behavioral principles, in reading instruction, arithmetic, and language. The purpose of these courses is to give you the rationale for the techniques that you use in the morning. Also, you'll have a course in instructional programming aimed at making you a good critic and analyst of instructional programs. During the second year of training, you will be responsible for training at least one new trainee. You will also work on 'troubleshooting projects.' You will go into a classroom where some of the kids are having problems. You will diagnose the problem, specify the remedy, and teach the kids. You'll have help if you need it. We have an obligation to provide effective instruction, so we're going to see to it that the kids get taught."

Next, Doris introduced the three other trainers who would work with the incoming trainees. All looked a little too young to Linda. She noted that there were four trainers to work with twenty-six students—one trainer for every six and a half students.

After introducing the others, Doris said, "Next Monday you're going to sit down and work with first-grade kids who are beginning in school. To have the skills that you need to do the job, we're going to have to practice a great deal. Before this week is over, you're going to feel that you've been put through a mill. But remember, the only way you're going to learn the kind of behaviors that you'll need to work with beginning children is to practice, practice, practice."

Focus on Teaching Behavior

Doris passed out a stack of papers to each trainee. "These are tasks from the instructional program you will use for teaching reading," she explained. "We're going to practice presenting each of these tasks."

Linda looked over the first task. It said:

Teacher: Motor—boat. [Pause] Say it fast.
Children: Motorboat.

Doris said, "Tasks that are identical to this are presented every day during the first thirty lessons of the program. In the task you have, the word is *motorboat*. However, you can use any word you want in its place. The format is always the same. You say the word slowly; then you tell the children to 'say it fast.' In the instructional program, the say-it-fast words are sequenced so that the children start out saying very easy words, such as *motorboat*. Later, more difficult words like *sister, money,* and *if* are introduced. The children will do five or six different words a day."

One of the trainees asked, "What's the purpose of this task?"

Doris said, "The idea is to prepare the children for what they will be expected to do later on. In this reading program the children will decode words by sounding them out. To sound out the word *man*, they will say, 'Mmmmaaaannnn.' Then they will put the parts together and 'say it fast.' The say-it-fast skill is one that they will need in order to read, so we teach say-it-fast *orally* before the children begin reading. In that way, all children will have the blending skill they need."

Another trainee asked, "Can't all kids do that say-it-fast thing?"

"Not all of them," Doris said. "In fact, if you find a first-grader who can't read the word *man,* for example, present the task to him orally. Say, 'Listen: mmmmaaaannnn. . . . Say it fast.' He probably won't be able to do it, even after you show him what you want him to do. Kids often don't have highly developed say-it-fast skills when they enter the first grade."

After Doris had answered several other questions she said, "We're going to practice presenting this task, so that you'll be able to *teach* say-it-fast to the slowest kids. That means that we have to work on a lot of picky details."

During the next hour Linda and the other trainees did nothing but practice that task. First Doris demonstrated the task. "You hold your hand out in front of you as if you're stopping traffic. Then you close your eyes and put your head down. You say, 'Motor—boat. . . . Say it fast.' You open your eyes and look up after you say, 'Say it fast.' You also move your hand down as a signal to the children to respond."

Doris demonstrated the task again and told the trainees to do it with her. She cautioned them about holding their hands still before saying, "Say it fast." Again and again, Doris and the trainees presented the task together. Linda felt a little silly.

"Let's try it again. Remember, hold your hand absolutely still until after you say, 'Say it fast.' Here, let me show you what some kids will do if you move your hand after you say, 'Motor,' the way some of you are doing. Carol, you be the child."

One of the other trainers stood in front of Doris. Doris said, "Watch what Carol does when I move my hand. Listen: Motor . . ." Doris moved her hand down.

"Motor," Carol said.

"Now we've created a problem," Doris said. "If you hold your hand still and don't look at the kids, they won't jump in. After you say, 'Say it fast,' you move your hand to signal them to respond."

And so they practiced again and again. "You've got the hand under control pretty well," Doris said. "But you're not pausing long enough after you say, 'Motor—boat.' Here's a rule: Always pause before giving the children a signal to respond. 'Say it fast' is a signal to respond. So you always pause before that signal for at least a second."

One of the trainees asked, "Won't it make it harder for the children if you pause before 'Say it fast'?"

"No," Doris said. "It will make it much easier. It will help the children to isolate the signal from the rest of the task. Also, it will set things up for corrections. We'll get into that a little later. You'll see what I mean then."

Linda and the other trainees practiced the task again. Linda felt that Doris had made an understatement when she'd said that the trainees would work on picky details.

Finally Doris said, "Let's break up into groups of three. Everybody in each group take turns at playing teacher while the others play the kids."

The groups of three formed. Linda found herself in a group with a young man and a woman. The woman took the teacher's part first. Linda decided that she would play the part of a child who wasn't very interested in the proceedings. When the woman said, "Say it fast," Linda said nothing.

Carol, the other trainer, walked over to Linda and said, "No mistakes now. We'll work on them later. Right now we just want to get the basic task down."

Linda felt that the rules were a bit restrictive, but she played the role of a tractable child. After the woman had presented the task again, Carol said, "You're moving your hand when you say the word slowly. Try it again. Hold your hand absolutely still until after you say, 'Say it fast.'"

The woman blushed. "Well, here I go again," she said, and she repeated the task.

"That's a lot better," Carol said.

Linda felt embarrassed when it was her turn to present and noticed that her hand trembled slightly when she tried to hold it still. She was surprised afterward when Carol said, "Not bad."

After everybody in Linda's group of three had presented the task twice (the second time with the word "ice—cream"), Doris said, "Okay, you can stop now."

One of the trainees said, "I find it difficult to present this stuff to adults. It would be different if we had kids."

Doris said, "It would be different, but I'm not sure that you would do any better with kids. When you work with kids, you'll make the same mistakes that you'll make right here. But you'll have many more problems to worry about that you'll have to attend to on the spot. Some of the children may not attend. They make mistakes. What you're doing now is really quite easy compared to working with kids. Let me show you one of the things the kids may do when you present say-it-fast the first time. Carol, you play the child." Doris held out her hand, looked down, and said, "Motor—boat. . . . Say it fast," she signaled.

Carol said, "Motor—boat."

"You've got to correct that mistake. How would you do it?"

One trainee volunteered. "I'd tell her, 'Motorboat.'"

Doris said, "That seems like a reasonable correction, but it won't work well with low-performing children. Let me show you what you might observe four months after say-it-fast has been introduced if the teacher merely gives the children the answer when they make the mistake. The kids are still working on the first say-it-fast tasks. They are completely confused.

"Teacher: 'Sis—ter. . . . Say it fast.'

"Children: 'Sis—ter.'

"Teacher: 'Sister.'

"Children: 'Sister.'

"Teacher: 'Good.'

"On every say-it-fast task, the same thing happens.

"Teacher: 'Ice—cream. . . . Say it fast.'

"Children: 'Ice—cream.'

"Teacher: *'Icecream.'*

"Children: 'Icecream.'

"Teacher: 'That's right.'

"Why doesn't the correction work?"

The other woman from Linda's group of three said, "They're just imitating what the teacher says."

"Right," Doris said. "Why are they doing that?"

"Because the teacher tells them that they're doing it right."

"Good observing," Doris said. "The teacher has taught the kids that if they just keep saying the words the way she says them, she'll tell them that they're doing it the right way. Their original problem was that they didn't know what the *signal* 'Say it fast' meant and the teacher didn't do anything to demonstrate its meaning."

Linda said, "Do children really make that kind of mistake? It seems hard to believe."

"Starting next Monday, you won't have to take my word for it," Doris said. "You'll probably have a couple of kids—maybe more—who make that mistake. And by then you'll know how to correct the mistake so that it doesn't recur day after day. In fact, you can help me demonstrate the correction. Come up here and stand next to Carol." As Linda walked up to the front of the room, she heard a smattering of applause.

Doris said, "I'll present the task to Carol. She'll make the mistake. I'll correct the task the right way. First I'll use Linda as model. Then I'll present the task to Carol again. Listen: Motor—boat. . . . Say it fast."

Carol: "Motor—boat."

Doris: "Say it fast. Say it fast. Watch Linda. She can really say it fast. Linda's turn: Motor—boat. . . . Say it fast."

Linda: "Motorboat."

Doris: "Good. That's saying it fast. Linda's turn again. Listen: Motor—boat. . . . Say it fast."

Linda: "Motorboat!"

Doris: "Good." To Carol: "Your turn to say it fast. Motor—boat. . . . Say it fast."

Carol: "Motorboat."

Doris turned to the trainees. "When a child makes the mistake of not saying the word fast, you can assume that he doesn't know the meaning of the signal 'Say it fast.' The correction that we just demonstrated works because it demonstrates what the signal means, how it works, and what kind of response it calls for."

Doris, Carol, and Linda demonstrated the correction again. Doris then directed the other trainees to say Doris' lines with her as she repeated the correction. Doris presented the correction at least a dozen times. Each time she called the group's attention to one of the details in the presentation. After the group had practiced the correction with Doris at least seven times, Doris said, "You've got to watch your pacing. It's one of the most important assets of an effective teacher. As soon as the model has demonstrated how to respond to the task, you've got to go back to the kid quickly: 'Your turn, Motor—boat.' Don't pause after saying, 'Your turn,' or the kid will just say 'motorboat' before you can present the task."

Analyzing Mistakes

The first day's session ended at three-thirty. The next day, Doris reviewed these tasks and the trainees practiced them over and over. Doris then said, "We're going to work on basic corrections now. Remember, a child is corrected when you can present the original task or any similar task with the child making no mistakes." Doris explained that there are three types of basic corrections, because there are three types of basic mistakes that beginning kids make:

1. A signal mistake—the child doesn't understand the meaning of the signal you give him.
2. An information mistake—the child understands the signal but lacks the information needed to respond appropriately. If you are asked, "What's the common

name for Quercus trees?" you understand what is being asked. You understand the signal. You may not respond properly, however, because you may lack information about the meaning of *Quercus.*

3. A motor mistake—the child is incapable of producing the response called for by the task. If you are told to do a back somersault in the air and land on your feet, you understand the signal. But you probably wouldn't perform because you can't produce the response called for by the task.

Doris illustrated each of the basic mistakes by presenting a series of problems to the group. She then reviewed the examples that gave the trainees problems. Finally she passed out some mimeographed problems, each of which specified the task the teacher presented and the mistake the child made. The trainees were to indicate whether each mistake was a signal mistake, an information mistake, or a motor mistake.

"When the kid makes a mistake, you have to decide whether he understood the meaning of the signal. If he didn't, you'll use the signal correction we worked on the other day. If he did understand the signal, help him produce the appropriate response."

Linda and the other trainees spent the rest of the day working on specific corrections. On Wednesday and Thursday, they continued to work on the tasks that would appear in the first part of the reading program. Friday was the last day of "preteaching" training. On Monday, Linda and the others would begin teaching. Linda had a feeling of uncertainty about whether she would be ready.

Final Preparations

Carol opened the Friday session by showing a video tape of several teachers presenting tasks to a group of five to eight beginning children. Carol stopped the tape at different places and pointed out specific techniques the teachers were using. "The first thing is to seat the children so that all can see the material. If you're in doubt, hold the book at the level of your eyes and see if you can see all of the kids' eyes. If you can't, they can't see the book. Place the low-performing kids in the middle of the group, right in front of you. Don't let them sit on the ends of the group. Remember, the farther the kids are from you, the more they will tend to go off task. You should be able to reach out and touch every kid. If you can't, they're too far away. But since the kids on the end will tend to have more behavior problems even if you can touch them, place the highest performers there."

One teacher on the tape opened the session with the "Stand up" game. Carol demonstrated the game and explained how it can be used to get children on task. "We're doing a study now that shows how important pacing is. With one group of children, the teacher pauses three seconds between tasks. With the other group, she pauses one second between tasks. The kids in the one-second situation are on task five times as frequently as the other kids. If you have good pacing—if you move fast at the right times—the kids will be much easier to manage."

Carol went over other basic rules of managing children, concluding with "Just remember, kids are not china dolls. They won't be traumatized for life if you tell them to turn around or to talk louder. Don't be afraid of them. On the other hand, don't be afraid to tell them that they're doing a good job when they're trying."

For the remainder of the day, Linda and the other trainees worked on the first lesson from the reading program that they would be using on Monday. They practiced the say-it-fast tasks, the sequencing tasks, and the sound-identification tasks all afternoon, working on such details as moving to the next task quickly, correcting mistakes, dealing with different types of possible behavior problems.

Learning by Doing

When Linda woke up on Monday morning, she felt scared. In the back of her mind was a sweaty-palmed fear. "I can't do it. I don't want to take the responsibility for teaching kids. I'm not ready."

Two hours later, Linda taught her first group of children. They looked terribly small to her. She presented the first say-it-fast task, and to her surprise two of the children in the group repeated the word slowly, just as the trainees had practiced it. Linda used one of the girls in the group who had said it fast to serve as the model. The correction seemed to work. "Good saying it fast," Linda said.

She presented another say-it-fast task. Nearly all of the children responded to her signal. "Good work," Linda said. The children smiled and Linda moved on to the next task.

When she was about halfway through the lesson, she noticed that Doris was standing next to her. After a few minutes Doris went to observe one of the other trainees in the room.

"You've got to watch two things," Doris said at the end of the period. "Your pacing is a little slow. And your criterion is soft. Don't tell the children they've done a good job until all of them have done a good job. Don't be afraid to repeat a task. Tell the kids, 'Not bad. Let's do it again. This time everybody say it.' If you don't maintain a hard criterion, some kids will learn that they can receive praise for doing nothing. They'll start giving you trouble in about three days."

Linda agreed that she would work on those points, but she felt that Doris was carping.

On the second day the children performed well. Linda praised them. They smiled and worked hard. The third day, the kids seemed indifferent. About halfway through the lesson, Billy pulled a toy truck from his pocket and started to play with it.

"Put it away, Billy," Linda said, but Billy didn't put it away. He ran it up and down his leg. "Give it to me," Linda said.

"It's mine," Billy said.

Linda reached for it.

"It's mine," Billy said. He turned around in his chair, concealing the truck.

Linda stood up. "Give it to me, Billy." She noticed that the girl at the other end of the group was crying. "What's the matter?" Linda said.

"He hit me," the girl said, pointing to one of the boys, who was denying it by shaking his head vigorously.

"Why did you hit her?" Linda said to the boy.

By now Billy was on the floor, playing with his truck. "Rrrrrr," he said as he scooted the truck along the floor.

After that, everything seemed to escalate. Linda managed to get the children back on task, but they erupted again after a few moments. The rules about handling kids flashed through Linda's head, but there were too many rules, too many kids, too much going on at the same time. She wanted to say, "Forget it," and run out of the room.

At some point during the third behavior episode, Doris came into the room. Linda shrugged.

Doris smiled, sat down next to Linda, picked up a piece of chalk and said, "I've got chalk. Who wants it?" Even as the kids were answering, Doris was talking. "Here's how you get it. Go fast. Ready. Stand up. . . . He's got it." She handed a piece of chalk to one of the boys. "Sit down. . . . Stand up. . . . Sit down. . . . Close your eyes. . . . She's got it for keeping her eyes closed. Now we're going to do some tough stuff. For chalk. Go fast and get some chalk." Doris wrote *m* on the board. "Everybody, open your eyes. . . . What sound is this? . . . Couldn't hear you. I've got a bad ear. Again. . . ." Doris was talking like a machine, very fast. "Okay, okay, moving on. Get ready. . . . Come on, guys, you can talk louder than that. Again. . . . Come on, again. Watch me. *Mmmmmmmmm.* That's what I call loud. Your turn. . . ." She passed out small pieces of chalk as the children responded. Billy, the girl and all the others were on task.

Doris went on for about five minutes. Then she stopped. "I'm tired. Who wants to be teacher? Everybody who does a good job on this next task gets to be teacher."

Everybody did a good job and everybody had a turn at being teacher. Doris prompted the "teachers." They loved it.

After the period was over, Doris said, "That's called talking over the kids. You talk and you move so that the kids can't interrupt you. They can't distract the other kids, particularly if you're giving out reinforcement. They'll play the game and you never have to call attention to their behavior."

"I don't know that I can do that," Linda said. "It looks exhausting."

"You *can* do it. It may be exhausting, but it's less exhausting than spending half of your time trying to manage the kids and get them on task. Don't be soft on your criterion. Let them know exactly how you expect them to respond. Show them. Then hold them to it. If you do, it will mean something to them when you tell them that they've done a fine job."

After that day, Linda had more respect for Doris. Doris didn't say, "I told you so."

Formal Studies

During the afternoon, Linda took courses based on the theory of engineering desired changes in kids. One course focused on managing and reinforcing children. The general principle expressed was: your behavior affects their behavior. A second course had to do with instructional programming. For one assignment, Linda and the others were required to evaluate the way fractions were introduced in one of the more widely used new-math programs. After noting the various misrules in the program and the holes (skills assumed to be present but never taught in the program), Linda and the others wrote a "patch-up" program that would make the program more teachable to more children.

Linda took courses in teaching beginning reading, arithmetic, and language, where she learned more about the rationale of effective instruction. She learned how to test and diagnose problems that children may have, and she practiced critical tasks from these programs. She learned about advanced corrections that are appropriate when the children have already been taught basic skills. She realized that reacting to the responses of the children is the hardest thing for a teacher to learn. When the kids answered correctly, things went smoothly. When they made mistakes, Linda's first impulse was to overlook the mistake and go on. She knew that she had to react *now,* but it sometimes took a few moments to think about what she should do. Linda already realized that the difference between her teaching and that of Doris had to do with the ability to react quickly and appropriately to the children's responses.

"Advanced corrections," Doris explained, "are based on the idea that when the child makes a mistake, he often tells you precisely what he has confused with what. When you tell the child to pick up a pencil and he picks up a piece of chalk, he is letting you know that he has two tasks confused. If you simply show the child the right way to do it, he may still be confused. He may not know under what conditions he is supposed to perform the act of picking up the chalk. The idea behind advanced corrections is to show him the *difference* between the task that you presented and the task he responded to correctly."

Doris then explained how to execute advanced corrections. First you tell the kid what he did correctly and contrast it with what you told him to do. "You picked up the *chalk*. But I told you to pick up the *pencil*." Next you firm the child on both of the tasks: "Pick up the chalk," and "Pick up the pencil." Linda and the others practiced executing the correction. Doris said, "You've got to be able to run these corrections until they become a natural part of your teaching behavior."

During the year, Linda worked very hard and she began to

realize that Doris was an amazingly useful source of information about how to do things the right way. Near the end of the year, Linda felt that she had managed to put it all together. She liked the kids and they liked her.

Teaching Low-performing Children

During Linda's senior year she continued to teach in the morning. She was assigned two groups of children, one labeled "retarded," the other "emotionally disturbed." As Doris said, "When you have the skills necessary to teach the kids that are tough to teach, you can teach *any* kid any subject. These kids will show it all to you." Linda also supervised two incoming trainees. One of them had very poor pacing and a soft criterion. "I'm going to tell you what you've got to work on," Linda said to the trainee, "and, believe me, I know. I had the same problem."

The group of retarded children that Linda taught progressed over one year in reading achievement and over one year in arithmetic achievement. The "emotionally disturbed" children outperformed the retarded children by a slight margin. In one year Linda had done more as a teacher than Mary did in six years of teaching. At the end of the year the state certified Linda and her classmates in the experimental program, as well as the several thousands like Mary who went through the traditional teacher-training program.

The program that Linda went through is capable of teaching nearly every student who is willing to work hard enough to master the hundreds of detailed skills needed to teach low-performing children.

Are the Colleges Ready to Teach?

If Mary had gone through this course, she too would have become an expert teacher. The program would have allowed her to "discover" through working with children. It would have given a sharp focus to that set of activities called teaching. Finally, it would have clarified her responsibility and demonstrated that Andys and Jimmys can be taught if the teacher has the skills called for by the assignment.

Linda's teacher training is relatively expensive and unpopular. The services of three trainers and two professors (who taught the afternoon theory courses) were needed to train twenty-six students in Linda's class. Some professors in Linda's institution have suggested that the cost of such training makes it impractical. This suggestion is naïve. If Linda's instruction is uniformly effective and the statutory programs are ineffective, the major issue is: Do we want professionals working with our kids or do we want Marys?

Actually, the reluctance of colleges to engage in the kind of training Linda received has more to do with philosophy than cost. The typical college obviously doesn't understand teaching and is incapable of training for it.

Perhaps the following story will illustrate the fear that colleges of education have about effective instruction of their students.

Our project, the Engelmann-Becker Follow-Through model, had been affiliated with the University of Illinois. We had conducted an experimental graduate training program which was funded for three years by the Carnegie Corporation. When it became apparent that the college of education "was not ready" to incorporate any of the training procedures into either special education or elementary education, we decided to move the project to a university that was more interested in effective teacher training. We wrote letters and contacted seven universities that expressed the most interest in being relevant, doing something to serve the community, etc. Our project was funded with a U.S. Office of Education grant of nearly one million dollars a year (which meant a substantial amount of "overhead" revenue to the sponsoring university). We indicated to all of the universities that we would move the entire project to their premises if they would allow us to conduct an undergraduate training program (like the one Linda went through) that led to certification. We were rejected or ignored by all but one of the institutions contacted. The most incredible reply came from Temple University, which had gone on record about doing something for the community. After a few phone calls and a letter, a dean wrote that the staff in two departments had voted *unanimously* not to allow our project to move to their campus.

Linda Is a Threat

The message conveyed by this and similar stories is that the colleges of education, as they are currently established, do not have a very strong commitment to actually train teachers to tackle real problems of instruction. Where does all of this leave Linda? It leaves her, unfortunately, as a threat to the other teachers in her school. She does not buy the party line. When a teacher says, "I always say that if the children don't read, they're not ready," Linda does not follow the protocol of nodding with agreement. She is likely to say, "I always say that they'll learn if you can teach them." The other teachers are suspicious of Linda. They don't recognize that she saves the community thousands of dollars every year by teaching children who would otherwise go into special classes. They don't seem to be aware that she is saving the Jimmys and Andys from the agony that they would experience if they weren't successfully taught.

Even the principal finds himself in a state of "ambivalence" about Linda. Parents of the lower-performing children often call and tell him what a beautiful thing Linda has done by teaching their child who had been diagnosed as unteachable. On the other hand, he hears complaints from other teachers about the noise in Linda's classroom. Linda creates friction, and the principal's goal is to maintain "harmony" among the staff members. It doesn't matter whether the children are failing, so long as there is harmony.

If this description seems exaggerated, let me assure you that it isn't. I've known perhaps fifty Lindas—teachers who go into schools and provide demonstrations of teaching that exceed anything that had ever been done in the school. In most cases the Lindas weren't recognized as saviors or mentors. They were treated as a foreign body that had to be removed. It is Mary who is recognized by the school system as the good teacher.

6

Instructional Programs

The Role of a Program

A teacher is no better than the instructional program she uses. A traditionally trained teacher is highly dependent upon instructional programs because she has received no training in constructing effective programs. In fact, she probably can't discriminate between an effective and an ineffective program. Teachers like Linda also depend upon instructional programs.

And the program relies on a teacher to transform written exercises, instructions, and illustrations into teaching. With poor teaching, the exercises specified in even the best instructional program will be sterile and ineffective. There are significant differences in instructional programs, however. The best way to see the difference is to contrast the beginning reading program that Mary uses with the one that Linda uses.

Let's look at the Harper & Row Basic Reading Program, a traditional basal that had been adopted by the state of California for use in all regular classrooms. The children are introduced to reading through four pre-primers, the first of which is titled *Janet and Mark*. The teacher's guide outlines in some detail the procedures for presenting each lesson. The first lesson presents three words: *Janet, Mark, and.* All three of them contain the letter *a;* however, the *a* makes a different sound in *Mark* than it does in *and* and *Janet.* The words *Janet* and *Mark* are associated with pictures. The teacher is instructed to tell the children, "Let's talk about what Janet is doing," and later to lead pupils to discover that Janet's hair is red and her eyes are brown. The word *Janet* is presented in the context of a discussion about Janet, which may imply to some children that the picture somehow gives a clue to the word. The teacher suggests that the discussion of Janet is a part of decoding the word. Although the teacher is instructed to trace the *J* in *Janet* and to call the children's attention to it, the teacher presents the word as a sight word. She doesn't show the children that the *n* and the *t* in the word also have a function.

After discussing the picture of Mark, the teacher introduces "Janet and Mark." She is instructed to say, "People we meet in books are called characters. In this picture you see two characters you have just met. Who are these children? Their names are right here under the picture." Later she tells them, "Perhaps you noticed this little word joins the names *Janet* and *Mark.* This word says *and.* We call *and* our joining word. Let's use the joining word and join some other people's names." The teacher is then to call two children to the front of the group and "hold the word card *and* between them."

If you want to play the game of a program analyst, ask yourself: Could the children possibly be misled by this presentation? Is it possible for them to misinterpret what a character is or what the word *and* is and does? The basic rule for constructing effective instructional programs is that each teaching demonstration must be consistent with only a single interpretation—the right one. If the children can possibly derive a misinterpretation, the demonstration will fail with some children. Is *and* called a joining word because it physically joins? Is it possible that any three-letter squiggle can function as a joining word? Are characters only children? What evidence do we have from the responses of the children that they understand what a character is?

For the next part of the first lesson, the teacher introduces the notion of initial consonants. She is instructed to say, "There is someone here whose name begins with the same sound as *Janet*. Listen as I say 'Jim . . . Janet.' Was I right?" The teacher continues to present such names as Jerry, John, Joel, Jane, Judy, and Julie. Let's apply our single-interpretation rule. Since all of the words presented begin with the *J* sound, we have no way of knowing whether the children can discriminate between words that begin with *J* and words that begin with something else. We have no way of knowing whether the children understand that each of the *J* words actually begins with the *J* sound. For all we know, they would contend that any word containing a *J* sound (such as edge) *begins* with a *J* sound. Neither Jimmy nor Andy had a firm understanding of the "sound the word begins with" by the time they completed the third grade. Like the other children who are exposed to the Harper & Row series, they have worked with initial consonant sounds from their first day of reading instruction.

During the second lesson, the teacher introduces the pre-primer. She presents the concept of the title. She briefly explains the meaning of the words *author* and *publisher*. She reviews the initial consonant sound *J*. And she works on noun-verb sentence patterns.

The third lesson introduces new words. The children read four pages from their pre-primer. The text: "Come, Mark. Come, Mark, come. Come here, Mark. Come here. Come here, Mark. Come and jump. Come and jump, jump, jump. Here I come, Janet. Here I come. Jump, jump, jump." The illustration shows a sequence in which the children take a skip rope to a playground and jump rope.

Many of the words that have been introduced are irregular. The *o* in *come* makes a short *u* sound. The *e* in *here* makes a long *e* sound, while the *e* in *Janet* makes a short *e* sound. The *a* in *Mark* is actually a short *o* sound. Within the next lessons, the children will be introduced to the new words *I, ride, can, my, go, see, the, down, socks*. The sequence might strongly discourage a child from "discovering" that the letters in a word generally convey the sounds one produces when he says the word. *Go* contains a long *o; socks* contains a short *o; come* contains a different *o. I, ride,* and *my* contain a long *i* sound.

Basic Facts of Instructional Programming

By the time the children have been in the reading program two weeks, they have received instruction on keying on the beginning letters of the word. From the teacher's guide:

> "When I look at the word *Janet,* I like to keep my eyes not only on the capital *J,* but on this letter also." Indicate and trace the *a.* "Then, when I write [write Ja——], you will tell me to finish the word ——." Finish the word *Janet.* Write Ja—— on the board several times, directing attention to the *a.* Finish the word *Janet* each time the name is suggested.

By now the children have been exposed to capital letters and the rule that proper names begin with capitals. They have done exercises with prepositions. They have engaged in exercises in which they use different intonations to signify anger, happiness, etc.

The Harper & Row series is a typical sight-reading basal, characterized by a weak identification of the skills the children need. Like most sight-reading programs, it has a little of everything—discussion, rules of English, and training. However, it lacks a focus. The more critical skills are often lost in a morass of activities. The naïve child may well come away with serious misrules. He may try to figure out the word from the picture. He may think that the words are spelled in an arbitrary fashion. He may fail to learn the meaning of "the beginning of the word." He has not been shown that the *J* makes a *J* sound and that each letter in the word ideally directs one to say a sound. He is supposed to discover this relationship for himself.

Here are some basic facts that the Harper & Row program fails to recognize:

1. A picture cannot indicate a word. It is impossible to construct any picture so that it does more than suggest possible words. Discussing the picture before reading the words suggests to some children that such analysis of the picture is an integral part of decoding.

2. Words are not identified by looking at the first two letters. They are identified by looking at all of the letters and by understanding that the order of the letters ideally dictates the order of sounds one produces when saying the word.

3. Verbally rich instructions do not teach. The elaborate explanations suggested in the teacher's guide are acceptable for only a percentage of children in the first grade. These explanations discriminate against the children who can't understand them.

4. When the skills in the program are not carefully sequenced, some children won't learn generalized skills. They will memorize bits and pieces. It is relatively easy to teach exceptions after a child has learned a general rule or skill. It is relatively easy to teach children that the letter *a* makes sounds other than *aaa* (as in *and*) after the children have learned the general function of the letter *a*. It is difficult to demonstrate that the *a* is not arbitrary and has no function in a word, if the first words containing *a* have different sounds.

5. The teacher has no way of knowing whether the children have mastered a particular skill if she doesn't receive feedback on the performance of *each* child. A "discussion" is a weak feedback device. It provides information about a few children but not about the many who don't "contribute."

Dewey Endorsed the Look-Say Method

There is considerable evidence to show that the look-say or sight method of reading doesn't work as well as more highly structured approaches. Yet most schools still use look-say programs to teach initial reading, because the method was strongly endorsed by progressive educators shortly after the turn of the century. John Dewey, who knew precisely nothing about instructing young kids, developed the slogan "Learn by doing." He noted that the look-say method of teaching reading was closer to "Learn by doing" than the more structured approaches. In the time that a child could learn to identify a dozen letters in the more structured programs, he could learn to identify a dozen *words* in the look-say method. He could read almost instantly. Although a number of studies have discredited the look-say approach, no amount of research seems capable of shaking the majority of traditional school administrators. Year after year, they purchase the look-say programs and somehow manage to rationalize the fact that one out of every four first-graders in the suburbs fails and is labeled dyslexic, and that perhaps one out of every two inner-city children fails in the first grade.

Those who make the decisions about instructional programs don't seem to realize that although you can teach children to identify the words *Janet, see, I,* and *Mark* as "sight" units with very little difficulty, the children will begin to make mistakes as soon as we introduce another word that begins with a capital *M.* They will probably call the new word *Mark,* whether the word is *Mary, May,* or *Mike.* If there were no words "similar" to each other in configuration, the look-say method would work. Unfortunately, there are hundreds of words that look similar. The only way to distinguish between them is to focus on the elements, the letters, in each. They explain why one word is *Mark* and the other is *Mike.*

There Is No Substitute for Careful Instruction

The look-say approach works with a fairly high percentage of children. In an average group of middle-class kids, we could expect about three fourths of them to master beginning reading by the end of the first year. The one out of four children in that average classroom who does not learn, however, represents a substantial and unnecessary loss. A highly structured reading program that would be clear to the children and precise for the teacher would teach these children beginning reading skills. In response to the need for such a program, Elaine Bruner and I wrote one—DISTAR Reading. The original version of the program has a number of faults, but it provides the teacher with the kind of specific directions that she needs to teach each of the basic prereading skills rather than merely expose children to these skills. The program has come under a great deal of attack, particularly from college professors who charge that the program is mechanistic and stifles the creative impulses of the teacher. Creativity is not a substitute for careful instruction, a point that was dramatized several years ago in an Eastern city.

At that time we were working with the staff in several of the district's schools. One evening a reading supervisor who was not participating in the program, but who worked in one of the participating schools, engaged me in a discussion that quickly turned into a heated argument. She insisted that the only way to teach children was with a basal system and not with radical programs like DISTAR. She was quite knowledgeable about instructional programs. After the argument had gone on for half an hour, a young teacher in our program who had been quietly observing the proceedings turned to the supervisor and said, "Myra, you probably know a hundred times more about reading than I do. I just got out of college last year. I don't know anything about the various philosophies of how to teach. All I know how to do is to follow the instructions in the DISTAR program. It tells me what to say, and I say it—word for word. It tells me what to do, and I do it. I could study for years and not know as much about reading as you do, but I'll tell you one thing: I've seen your kids perform, and mine perform better."

The supervisor was a good teacher. She was a first-rate ham and had good instincts. The young teacher in our program had never worked with beginning readers before. Yet her statement about the performance was true. Her kids outperformed those of the knowledgeable supervisor. There have been a number of studies in which DISTAR has been compared to other programs. One school district near Sacramento, California, improved over fifty percent in reading performance, using DISTAR. Its schools had performed well below the average of California schools; now they are quite a bit above average. In another study, children in an Oregon school district were screened using a diagnostic test that was supposed to predict reading failure. The children who performed the lowest on the test were given DISTAR. By the end of the year the DISTAR kids were significantly ahead of the children who had been diagnosed as "ready" and who were placed in a traditional program.

Our work with twenty participating sites through the University of Oregon Follow Through model discloses that the poverty children in the program gain 1.4 years in reading skill (as measured by the Wide Range Achievement Test) for every year they are in school. The average performance of children who begin the program in kindergarten and proceed through the third grade is 5.0 grade levels in reading performance at the end of the third grade. Where the program has been well implemented (which is certainly not in every classroom of every site), all children read at least near grade level by the end of the third grade.

Reading as Decoding

Rudolph Flesch argued in the book *Why Johnny Can't Read* that reading is basically the act of decoding. Since the time the book came out in the fifties, educators have smarted over his argument. They counter that reading is communication, experience, comprehension, and a host of other things. Flesch was right. The central difference between hearing and reading is that one must decode written words when one reads. A person may not understand some of the words he hears, just as he may not understand some of the words that he reads. A person may not understand sentence forms that he hears. Similarly, he may not understand sentence forms that he reads. Just as a person is preempted from certain understanding of what he hears unless he actually hears the words that are said, a reader who reads the sentence "The house was red" as "The horse was red" is preempted from comprehending what the sentence said. He did not understand because he didn't take the first and most important step of decoding what was on the printed page. The first step in reading instruction—and the most important—must be that of decoding. Decoding skills are taught *first* in DISTAR. Reading comprehension skills are taught *after* the children have learned how to decode accurately.

One Symbol: One Sound

What are the skills that a child must have if he is to decode simple, regular words? Let's look at a word and analyze it to see what we have to know in order to read it:

mat

We're interested only in the skills needed to identify the complex sound *mat*, not necessarily to interpret the meaning of the word. The letters are signals for us to produce *sounds*. The letter names won't help us decode the word, no matter how rapidly we "blend" them. Say the letter names fast: *em-ay-tee—emmaytee*. They don't yield the word *mat*. However, the sounds do: *mmm-aaa-t—mat*. Since the letter sounds are essential to decoding, DISTAR teaches sounds, not letter names, when presenting new sounds at the rate of one every three or four days. Children can master the alphabet at a much faster rate; for children to learn how to manipulate each sound independent of the rote series, the rate must be slowed considerably. Below is the initial DISTAR alphabet.

a	m	s	ē	r	d
f	i	th	t	n	c	o
ā	h	u	g	l	w
sh	I	k	ō	v	p
ch	e	b	ing	ī	
y	er	x	oo	J	
ȳ	wh	qu	z	ū	

Such symbols as *th* and *ch* are designed to permit the children to read words that would otherwise be irregular. The word *ate* is written in the early DISTAR program as āte. The child can now treat the word as a perfectly regular word. At the same time, we can spell the word as it is conventionally spelled. The *e* on the end of the word is printed in smaller type, the smaller type indicating that the *e* is silent. Rule: You don't read the small letters. As the children become familiar with words that are spelled as they are pronounced, we can begin to introduce irregular words and move the child toward reading from conventional orthography. In words like *ate,* the long line over the *a* is dropped and the *e* is brought up to full size. Before the child begins to read regularly spelled words, he is facile at handling words in which each symbol is a signal for producing a particular sound.

Sequencing Events

Let's return to the word *mat* and analyze what else we must know to decode the word. Some educators have suggested that we have to teach left-right orientation, meaning by that some sort of "visual" rule. The skill involved is more complicated. We can read the word when it is written like this:

$$m$$
$$a$$
$$t$$

—indicating that what is referred to as left–right progression actually refers to the way in which we sequence the sound events that are signaled by the letters. Before the children in the DISTAR program work with tasks that involve sounding out words, they work with sequences of events that are easier than letter sounds. The teacher presents a sequence of two actions. For example, she may clap her hands and then slap her knees.

"I did it the right way," she tells the children. "Watch again." She repeats the sequence. Next she tells the children, "Do it with me." Children and teachers do the clap-slap sequence together several times. After each time they do the sequence, the teacher tells the children, "That's the right way."

The teacher now presents different sequences and asks the children if each is "the right way." She claps and then taps her head. "Is that the right way? . . . Show me the right way." She claps and then slaps her knees. "Is that the right way? . . . Show me the right way." Finally she reverses the clap-slap sequence, slapping her knees, then clapping. "Is that the right way?" Some naïve children say that it is. It is frightening to think of teachers in traditional programs referring to the "first letter," the beginning sound, and the word ending when the children may not be able to discriminate between a simple sequence and the sequence reversed.

Language of Instruction

After the children have had practice with a number of different action sequences, DISTAR teaches them the meaning of "first" and "then." The teacher presents a sequence, indicating that she did it the right way. The children perform the sequence. The teacher then repeats the sequence, an action at a time. "When I do it the right way, first I do this . . . and then I do this. When I do it the right way, first I do this. . . . Then what do I do? Show me." It probably comes as no surprise that some children repeat the entire sequence. These children are not stupid; they simply haven't been taught the convention for breaking a sequence into its parts.

After they have learned to isolate the action that follows the first action, they take the next step and work on tasks in which they show what the teacher did *first* when she did it the right way and what she did *then,* or next.

When the children are firm on the concept that a sequence is a sum of actions that can be broken into component actions, the children are introduced to an action "code." They are shown pictures of two actions with an arrow beneath the action: ⟶ In one exercise, the actions illustrated are a boy with his hand on his head and then a boy with his mouth open. "Let's follow the arrow and do what it tells us to do. . . ." The teacher points to each picture as the children produce the appropriate actions. "Everybody, what do we do first? Show me. . . . Then what do we do? . . ." By working on a similar series of illustrated action sequences, the children master the basic sequencing assumption involved in reading words.

Blending Skills

To read the word *mat,* or any other simple word, the child needs skills in addition to letter-sound skills and sequencing skills. After the child sequences the events *mmmm, aaa,* and *t,* he must have the "blending" skill necessary to telescope the sounds and put them together—*mat.* Since Andy did not have this blending skill, he found it impossible to identify words after he went through the procedure of sounding them out.

In DISTAR, the blending skill is called say-it-fast, the task that Linda and her trainees worked on so fervently during their first day of training. Say-it-fast is taught as an oral exercise starting on the first day of the program, long before children decode their first written words. The idea is to make sure that they have the blending skill before they are required to use it in the complex task of word reading, a basic programming procedure.

The sequence of say-it-fast first presents words that are easy to blend orally: *motor—boat; ham—burger; ice—cream.* After the children have mastered the easiest examples of say-it-fast, they work on more difficult blends: *can—dy, broth—er,* and so forth. Before they use say-it-fast to read words, they have worked

on the most difficult words, such as *mmmmmaaaaannnnn,
iiiiifffff,* and *mmmmmeeeee.*

Before encountering written words, the children are also
taught the converse of say-it-fast, which is "spell by sounds." The
teacher shows that orally presented words can be broken into
component sounds. "Spell *was* by sounds: wwwwwuuuuuuzzzz."
This exercise calls for words to be spelled as they are *pronounced,* not necessarily as they are written.

Rhyming

A final prereading skill is rhyming. We know that the word *mat*
rhymes with the ending *at.* With this knowledge we are in a
position to generalize when we encounter new words such as
zat, wat, clat, and *psycat.* Only a small percentage of beginning
readers have a firm understanding of rhyming. Initial rhyming
exercises in Distar are verbal. The teacher says, "Listen:
Rhymes with *ice—cream:* sss . . ." She signals for the children to
say the word: "Sisecream." "Rhymes with *ice—cream:* mmmm
. . . rrrr . . ." For about a month, the children work on similar
rhyming tasks, each word presented according to the same
format, "Rhymes with [word]: [initial sound] . . ."

Combining the Skills

When the children have completed the prereading program
(learning eight or nine sounds, mastering say-it-fast, symbol action games, and rhyming), they are "ready" to decode such words
as *mat.* The readiness program simply introduces skills directly
related to the decoding of regularly spelled words and provides
a great deal of practice in each skill. If the teacher makes sure
that the children are firm on each lesson in the program, all
children will be able to take the next step—that of using the
skills to decode simple words.

DISTAR ensures both that the children have mastered all of the component skills and the vocabulary necessary to follow directions on attacking simple words, and that the teacher can correct any mistake the children make.

In the first word-reading exercises, the program puts all of the skills together. The teacher points to the individual letters of the word as the children say them: "Mmmmaaaat." The children are taught not to pause between the sounds of the word when they sound it out. The reason is that the word *mmmmm-aaaaat* sounds much more like *mat* than the unblended word *mmm—aaa—t* does. When we say words, we don't pause between the sounds.

After the children have sounded out the word several times, the teacher says, "Say it fast." The teacher uses this presentation for all of the regularly spelled words presented in the program: *if, so, and, me, that.*

Correcting Mistakes

The children may make mistakes. They may misidentify sounds. They may fail to say the word fast after sounding it out. They make the mistake of identifying the word *mat* as *at*. If the children have been taught the prereading skills, the teacher can correct any mistake by referring to one of the previously taught skills. If a child fails to say a word fast after sounding it out, the teacher can change the task into a verbal say-it-fast task. "Listen, Henry: *mmmmmaaaat*. Say it fast. . . . Good. Now let's do it with the book. When I touch the sounds, you say them. . . ." The child sounds out the word; the teacher says, "Say it fast," and the child performs. The teacher didn't *tell* the child the word. He figured it out. The teacher merely prompted him by reducing the task to an oral one and then returned to the original printed word.

If the child identifies the word *mat* as *at*, the teacher says, "Rhymes with *at*," and touches the first sound of the word. This

format is familiar to the child. It is the rhyming format on which
he worked for weeks.

Decoding Irregular Words

If English were a regular language, the decoding phase of reading would virtually be completed at this point. All that would
remain would be to provide practice in handling words of more
than one syllable. But English is highly irregular. The letter *a*
does not make a single sound. It ranges from an *uh* sound to an
aw sound. Consider the *a* sound in these words: *about, ear, all,
art, act.* Irregular words are not presented until the child has a
firm grasp on regular words. Before he learns exceptions, he
learns the rule, or the way that words are ideally formed.

The problem in teaching irregular words is to make it clear
to the children that a word like *was* is not randomly spelled or
randomly pronounced. Every time we want to put the spoken
word "wuz" into print, we do so by writing *was*. Unless the
introduction of irregular words is handled carefully, children will
think that the introduction of irregular words is a license for
them to call any word anything at all. Children who tend to go
in this direction simply don't understand that a given irregular
word is always spelled the same way, but the spelling does not
correspond precisely to the word as it is spoken.

Irregular words are introduced very cautiously in Level 1
of DISTAR. The basic format calls for children first to sound out
the written word (making the appropriate sounds for each
letter): "Wwwwwwwaaaaaaasss." The teacher then says, "But
we don't say wwwaaasss. What do we say?" Children: "Wuz."

The purpose of the sequencing of irregular words is to make
the reading code as reasonable as possible to the child, rather
than making it appear random and nonsensical.

Reading Stories

As soon as the children have been taught their first regular words, they begin to read simple stories from take-homes. A take-home is not homework, but is a story that is read and mastered in class and then taken home so that the parents can note the child's progress and see on a day-to-day basis what is happening in school. The take-homes also increase the probability that the child will practice outside the classroom. When the parents see the child read, they may praise him, encourage him, and give him some kind of payoff for good reading. This is particularly important among parents of disadvantaged children who have seen some of their older children fail in school. For them it is exciting to see their youngster, who is perhaps in kindergarten, actually learning to read.

After completing the first level, the children can decode reasonably well. They can read sentences a word at a time without sounding out every word. They can answer simple questions about sentences that they have read, and make reasonable predictions about what may happen in a story.

Reading for Meaning: Drawing Inferences

Although comprehension activities are presented in the first-level program, the fundamental goal of Level 1 (which is generally completed in a school year or less) is to teach children decoding skills. Once they have these skills they are ready to embark on activities that teach them to comprehend with word-by-word understanding rather than with "general ideas." Perhaps the distinction between the two types of comprehension can be illustrated by referring to a group of tenth-grade children who are in Upward Bound, one of the federally funded programs of the sixties designed to prepare disadvantaged children for college. We presented the following passage to the kids:

> Tony stopped at the top of the ridge. He sniffed the air and kicked his hoof against the loose dirt several times. He was afraid. There was something in the air— something like the smell of a cat. But Tony knew that this cat was not like the cats back at the ranch. This cat was big and frightening.
>
> Tony felt Bill pull on the reins. "Let's go, Tony."
>
> But Tony did not go. He stood there and sniffed the air.
>
> "What's wrong, boy?" Bill said. Tony felt the jab of Bill's spurs. "Let's go, boy."
>
> But Tony stood there at the top of the ridge almost frozen.

The passage doesn't say that Tony is a horse. To determine what he is, you have to put the bits of evidence together— words and phrases such as "sniffed the air," "kicked his hoof," and "felt the pull of the reins." If somebody suggests that Tony is a man, you point out the bits of evidence in the passage that don't add up to Tony being a man.

The kids are able to read the passage, and they can usually indicate that Tony is a horse (or possibly a mule). However, they are unable to construct a case, using the words in the story, to defend their conclusions against a devil's advocate who suggests that Tony is a lion, a mouse, or a man.

These kids are the product of poor teaching. For them, comprehension involves getting the general idea, sort of understanding, unconsciously using at least some of the evidence presented in the passage, perhaps in injecting their own interpretation, but not recognizing that their conclusion is the product of the specific words the author put on that piece of paper. These children are handicapped when they attempt to discuss something they read and when they try to defend their interpretation of a textbook, a poem, or a newspaper article.

Attention to Details

The goal of DISTAR 2 is to teach children how to read defensively: to read with attention to the details of what is written, so as to be able to defend the interpretation they give by referring to the words in the passage. The vehicle used to teach this comprehension skill is called "read-the-items." A read-the-items exercise is a list of items that must be read carefully. For example, here are three consecutive items from one of the early read-the-items:

1. When the teacher says, "Stand up," hold up your hand.
2. When the teacher says, "Do it," pick up a white card.
3. When the teacher stands up, say "Stand up."

These are "low-probability" items, which means that there is no way a child can figure out what to do or under what conditions to do it unless he reads the item very carefully. He cannot cue from a picture, from the context, or from what he thinks the item will say after he has read only the first part of it.

The teacher assigns one item at a time. "Read item one to yourself. Raise your hand when you've read it."

The children read the item to themselves, and raise their hands.

The teacher then says, "Read it again to make sure you know *what to do* and *when to do it*. Then we'll play a game and see if I can fool you."

The children read the item again.

"Okay, let's play the game," the teacher says. She pauses. "Do it." If any of the children does something, the teacher says,

"I said, 'Do it.' Read item one out loud. Show me where it tells you what to do when I say, 'Do it.'" The children read the item and aver the item mentions nothing about what to do when the teacher says, "Do it."

"Let's see if I can fool anybody again. Get ready. . . ." The teacher stands up. No children respond.

"I couldn't fool you. Let's try again. Get ready. . . . Stand up."

Every child holds up his hand. "Couldn't fool you," the teacher says. "Everybody, read item one out loud."

The children read the item. They then go to the next item, read it to themselves, and see if the teacher can fool them.

The items on the children's worksheets become progressively more difficult as the children proceed through the program. Before long, the children are working such items as this: "4. When the teacher says, 'Go,' do what item 7 tells you to do." The children must refer to item 7, which says, "Pick up a red card and a yellow card."

Before the children complete the second level of the program, they work items more difficult than the example above. Since the program proceeds in small steps and allows for the teaching of the comprehension skills involved, all children can master these skills. The format of presentation allows the teacher to test whether the children are reading the items correctly, whether they are attending to the details of each item, and whether they are able to apply the "rule" specified in the item.

In addition to read-the-items, the Level 2 program includes stories and comprehension questions, similar to those in more traditional programs. The new vocabulary of these stories is light—that is, not many new words are introduced in the second-level program. The rationale for the light vocabulary load is to ensure that the children develop fluency. If the vocabulary is composed mostly of familiar words, the children tend to develop this set. They learn to feel that the words are familiar.

Textbook-Attack Skills

After completing Level 2 the children read well. They could succeed in any "basal" reader. Now the children are ready for the third level of the program.

To appreciate the rationale of the third-level DISTAR reading program, you have to understand the two most significant characteristics of the fourth grade: (1) most textbooks published for fourth-grade children are not written on the fourth-grade level, and (2) most reading programs do not prepare children for reading textbooks on any level.

We recently did an informal analysis of fourth-grade texts for sentence forms, vocabulary, and sentence length to determine the "grade level" of the material. Although I didn't analyze every published program, I worked with a fair sample, and not one was written on the fourth-grade level. Most were written on about the middle-sixth-grade level, with at least one written on the eighth-grade level.

Below are a few excerpts from fourth-grade texts. Note that they have not been selected as the most outrageous examples one can find. They are representative of passages found in most fourth-grade material.

A mixture is a material composed of two or more substances, each of which keeps its own characteristics. In a mixture, none of the substances put together have changed. Each molecule of each substance remains exactly as it originally was. No substance with a different combination of atoms is formed.

> [*Probing into Science,* published by American Book Company]

Aside from the fact that the description is less than compelling, consider that the language was designed for adults. The vocabulary and the sentences are certainly not designed for a child who doesn't yet understand that the weight of an object is independent of the size, that a steel ball dropped into water displaces an amount of water equal to the size of the ball. This passage could hardly be judged suitable for the average fourth-grader, who, according to the norms, has just mastered the basic 220 words that are supposed to appear most frequently in print.

Another example:

> Our experiment does not *prove* that division can be distributed over addition, because we tried only a few cases. However, it can be proved and you will, no doubt, do so when you are older. We will need to use this property when we divide greater numbers.
>
> [*Exploring Elementary Mathematics Patterns and Structure,* published by Holt, Rinehart & Winston]

The language is incredible. It would take a sophisticated mind to identify the "property" the author refers to in the last sentence. The exposition so thoroughly cloaks the meaning the author is apparently trying to convey that it would be presumptuous to suppose that a fourth-grader could handle it.

Another example:

> Long ago, the Dutch worked out ways of getting water from their land into the sea. Even if the sea never flooded the land, they would still need to drain water away from it. The land is so low that water from rain often stands on it.
>
> Canals have helped solve the problem. The Dutch have dug canals in which water can run from the fields. They have built other canals that are higher than the land round about. From these higher canals water can flow into the sea.
>
> [*Our Big World,* published by Silver Burdett]

In this example we are told that the land is low and that the high canals solve the problem. But how does the water get from the low land into the high canals? Either the land is not low or water flows uphill. Note such quaint expressions as "round about," which are not exactly everyday terms, and the loose references, such as "they" and "it" in the second sentence. The author obviously presupposes a sophisticated reader.

A final example:

Nouns and Pronouns:

What kind of word is the subject of a sentence? Look at the sentences below. Which word is the subject of the verb *cooked?*

Pauline cooked a delicious lunch.

When you ask, "Who cooked?" the answer is *Pauline.* Pauline is the subject of the sentence. Pauline is also the word that names the person who did the cooking.

Now look at this sentence. Which word names the person who did something?

The new president of our class spoke at the meeting.

When you ask, "Who spoke?" the answer is *president.* *President* is the word that names the person who did the speaking. *President* is the subject of the verb.

There is a name for words like *Pauline* and *president.* They are called NOUNS. A noun is a word that names a person, place, or thing. Not all nouns are subjects. Look at the sentence below.

Jane chose *Marion.*

The word *Jane* is the subject. But *Marion* is a noun, too. *Marion* names a person. That person, however, was not the one who did the choosing.

A noun is not the only kind of word that can be a subject. Sometimes the subject is a PRONOUN. A pronoun is a word used to take the place of a noun. Can you find the pronouns in the following sentences? Each one is the subject of a verb.

> *She* cooked a delicious lunch.
> *He* spoke at the meeting.
> *They* came to the party early.

The subject of a sentence is usually a noun or a pronoun.

> [*English 4: Language: Linguistics: Composition*]

This passage illustrates the incredible rate at which new concepts are introduced in most fourth-grade textbooks. From a one- or two-sentence explanation, phrased frequently in language that the children wouldn't understand if the explanation were presented orally, the children are expected to digest a new concept and then proceed immediately to another.

Textbooks as Punishers

Teachers who frequently complain about children who become "word callers," those who read the words with reasonable accuracy but fail to understand what they read, don't seem to recognize that the textbooks the children read are designed to reinforce word calling. Reading aloud several pages every day from a science text may prove to be punishing to the typical fourth-grader. It may not take him too long to discover that he isn't expected to understand. He sees that after he goes through the motions of saying the words (at least most of them) and looking at the picture, the teacher explains what he has read. He may never fully realize that she bases her explanation on the text passage he has "read." He learns, instead, that there is an order of events: first you call off the words; then the teacher explains. You never reread the passage and receive verification that the teacher's explanation precisely corresponds to the textbook explanation.

The Spiral Curriculum

Difficult material is not the only device used by traditional textbooks to unmotivate and confuse children. The traditional programs often follow what is called a "spiral curriculum," which is well designed to teach children that (1) they are not responsible for learning new material to mastery, and (2) they will not use any information they learn.

A spiral curriculum consists of a number of topics. In science, the topics include electricity and lightning, the human body, animal life, water and gases. Every year, these topics are presented to the children, with the discussion of each topic constantly becoming more sophisticated.

The spiral curriculum unintentionally teaches children that they are not required to master the material presented in the text. They quickly see that it is the frog pond (or biology) today and the air pressure tomorrow. Rarely are they required to use information presented in any unit, until the unit appears in the sequence next year. Many children, therefore, go through the motions of reading and trying to perform on their worksheets.

The Spiral-Teaching Philosophy

Teachers often learn behaviors that parallel the children's, realizing that within the three or four days allotted to the presentation of a topic they can't teach the children the material covered in the text. At best, they can "expose" children to the ideas in the text. It is enough for teachers to rationalize that no great problems result if the children are not taught a particular unit. They probably won't use this information in any of the units that follow.

In the typical English spiral curriculum, children are exposed to parts of speech, subject–verb agreement, giving and following directions, and rules of punctuation from the time they reach the third or fourth grade until they finish high school. Yet it is not uncommon to find eighth-grade children who don't know the difference between an adjective and an anteater. If we were to translate this fact into the time devoted to abortive teaching of adjectives, we would discover that a total of more than ten hours has been devoted to work on adjectives, with a questionable return.

The spiral curriculum doesn't work, because it doesn't show the children that they are accountable for using what they are taught. Ideally, the first step is to master the skill or information; the next is to use it.

The Reading Program—a Sharp Contrast

It is unrealistic to suppose that any reading program can prepare children for most current fourth-grade textbooks. However, it seems reasonable to suppose that children should be taught how to attack textbooks, and that this skill should be taught as part of the subject called reading.

When we look at the typical third- and fourth-grade reading programs, however, we discover that they don't attempt to teach children how to read text material. Children who have completed the fourth grade have often been exposed to an uninterrupted diet of fiction and poems in their reading circle, while in their other subjects they are expected to read traditional textbooks. Most of the "skills" presented in the reading circle are duplicated in other subjects. For example, the phonic rules that are introduced in reading are usually presented in the spelling or English program. Topics related to the use of reference material, syllabication, and poetry reading are also frequently duplicated.

The most compassionate justification for the focus on fictional reading in the third- and fourth-grade reading programs is that it provides children with an enjoyable interlude to offset the drudgery of working in the other subjects. This justification is not trivial; however, it doesn't change the basic fact that the children will be expected to perform in the other textbooks (which is not to say that this situation is justified.)

Teaching Textbook-Attack Skills

The Level-3 DISTAR program departs from tradition by emphasizing how to learn new information from textbooks. Here is the rationale: A child will do a variety of reading during his life, both fiction and nonfiction. If he has the basic comprehension and decoding skills demanded by interesting fiction selections, he will read these selections with a minimum of teaching. Not that he should continue to read fiction material. The point is that he doesn't have to be taught a great deal to handle fiction that is commensurate with his ability.

Most of what the child will later read, however, is nonfiction. The textbook is the major component of what he will read in school. In addition, much of what he will read for pleasure is nonfiction: newspapers, topical books, and instructions. Since nonfiction comprises most of his school reading and at least a part of his nonschool pleasure reading, textbook-reading skills seem to occupy a position of the greatest importance to the child who has mastered basic decoding and comprehension skills. A textbook-reading strategy involves (1) reading low-probability rules very carefully; (2) understanding that examples in which the rule is applied are not merely examples but examples *of the rule;* (3) organizing new information so that you can retain it and keep it from becoming confused with similar information; and (4) learning that text reading can be rewarding.

A child who has successfully completed the Level-2 DISTAR program has been taught to handle low-probability rules through the presentation of read-the-items. The next step is to teach the relationship between a rule and the examples of the rule. This is achieved in the Level-3 program by introducing a "deductive" format. A rule is presented at the beginning of a selection. Each time the rule is applied, the children are referred back to the rule, to show that the rule holds for all examples. A second safeguard is a test of the children's understanding. After reading each selection, the children are presented a series of questions that relate to the content they have read. Some items test the child's understanding of examples that were presented in the reading selection. Other items test his ability to apply the rule to examples not discussed in the reading selection. The only way the children can learn to perform consistently on these items is to apply the rule. The children learn very quickly that they will be "tested" on new applications of each rule. They learn that it is important to read each application carefully and to recognize it as an example of the rule.

Constant Review

The best way to help children to organize their understanding of information is to demonstrate to them that they are responsible for using the information. The Level-3 program provides this demonstration through daily review questions. After reading each of the daily selections, the children answer questions that refer to the selection they have just read. Following this set of questions is a set that refers to any of the concepts previously presented in the program. On Lesson 40 the child may be asked review questions that relate to Lesson 31 or perhaps Lesson 21. The review questions are sequenced so that they appear frequently. Throughout the year, most of the key review questions will appear at least ten times.

Another technique used to help children organize material is the unpredictable sequencing of the selections in the program. If there are four selections on a subject, not all four will be presented on consecutive days. Two may be presented on consecutive days, then there may be an interval of four or five days before the third pressure story appears. The third level of the program purposely scatters the selections in each "unit" so that children don't know what they will read on the following day. Perhaps tomorrow's selection will present a new topic. Perhaps it will extend a topic that has already been presented. To be prepared for the possibilities, the child learns to organize the information and concepts that have been presented. He learns that he will probably *use* every concept that has been taught. He therefore has a purpose for remembering and organizing information when it is presented.

The Best for the Last

In a traditional program, the typical ploy is to first present something that is supposed to be "meaningful" to the child. It is designed to seduce the child into learning a difficult concept. Theoretically, after his "interest" has been aroused, he will devour the material. It doesn't usually work that way. The child becomes interested. As he proceeds through the program, however, he learns that it actually wasn't as interesting as he had thought. In Level-3 DISTAR, the opposite tack is taken. The "payoff" or reinforcement selections come at the end, not at the beginning of the program. The purpose of these selections is to dramatize what the children have learned—to put it in the context of adventure and suspense.

The vehicle used to achieve this end is the cliff-hanging serial. For example, the last thirty-four selections in the program comprise one continued adventure that involves Al and Mike, two kids who hate school and who are doing poorly. In the first episode Al is walking home from school when he discovers a strange street that he never noticed before—Anywhere Street. Among the small shops on the street is one with an unusual sign in the window: "Go anywhere; see anything." The old man who owns the store tells Al that he can go anywhere—to the moon, to the bottom of the ocean, even inside the human body. "Go anywhere; see anything; and pay for your trip by passing a test on what you see." After some persuasion, Al consents to go on a trip. Al indicates that he would like to go fast. Suddenly the walls of the store seem to melt and Al finds himself at a racetrack with the old man. In front of them is a yellow racing car. After screaming down the track in the racing car, Al and the old man go on to something faster—a jet plane. They continue to move to faster vehicles until Al finds himself flying at the speed of light from the earth to the sun. The old man points out that they can go no faster and that it would take them over four years to fly to the nearest star. In this and the following Al and Mike episodes, the concepts dramatized are those the children have studied in the program.

Before the children read the Al and Mike stories, they have been taught facts about the distance of the earth from the sun, about miles per hour and the instrument used to gauge speed, about the speed of light and how long it takes light to travel from the sun to the earth. The purpose of the Al and Mike stories is not to teach new facts, but to make the facts "fat" and meaningful. When a child who has been properly taught reads the sequence, he can say to himself, "Oh, yes, I know that."

After a child has completed the Al and Mike series and has gone to the bottom of the ocean, inside the human brain, to the era of the dinosaurs, to the planet Uranus, and to a host of other places, he will appreciate the knowledge that he has, and he will see knowledge not merely as sterile bits but as something real, dramatic, and powerful. He will know that he has mastered something worthwhile. This is why the payoff comes at the end of the program, not the beginning.

Give All Children an Equal Footing

The content of the Level-3 program is "different." So are the procedures that the teacher follows. Part of every lesson is a "workcheck," conducted after the children have written answers to the worksheet for the lesson. The teacher assembles the children in a small group and spends about fifteen minutes going over each question on the worksheet. The children read each question aloud and then answer it orally. They mark on their worksheets whether they had the item correct. If more than one or two children miss a particular item, the teacher notes it. After she has gone through all of the worksheet items, she instructs the children to turn their worksheets over so that they can't see the items. She then orally presents all of the items that were missed by more than one or two children. She *teaches* each of these items. When the children leave the workcheck, they should be able to answer every item on the worksheet, even if they missed some of the items before. Tomorrow all of the children will start on the same footing. Every child will be prepared for the new information that will be presented. It is reasonable for a child to make mistakes on his workcheck; it is unreasonable for a teacher to mark these items, put a grade at the top of his paper, and never *teach* him the correct answers.

The rationale for the workcheck is very simple. If a child fails to master a concept that is presented today, he will be penalized when that concept is reviewed or when it appears again in a later selection. The workcheck is simple insurance that each child will not be penalized.

The Reference-Book Game

The Level-3 program has been criticized by traditional educators on the grounds that it requires children to retain information. The idiom of traditional education is that the children don't have to clutter their heads with information as long as they have reference books in which they can look up the answers. The traditionalists often fail to appreciate the degree of sophistication a child must have before he can use reference books efficiently. Not uncommonly, children turn to a book that cannot yield the answer they want because they don't know exactly what they are trying to look up. When asked what they are trying to find, they indicate that they can't understand a paragraph in the textbook, but they are unable to indicate what they hope to find in the reference book.

The paradox of the reference-book game is that the child must have basic textbook-reading skills before he can hope to handle reference books consistently. He must first be able to identify exactly what he doesn't know. He must state the problem to himself so that he knows in advance *what kinds of information will answer his question.* After he reads the answer, he must be able to remember it long enough to return to the original problem and note how the answer solves his problem. If either the original problem or the answer drops from his memory, the reference-book activity did not serve the child.

Children must become facile at organizing and retaining new information if they are ever to become intelligent in their use of reference books. Reference-book skills can be taught, but the first step is to make sure that the children have the information-processing skills that they need.

Breaking with a Sick Tradition

The DISTAR reading program is not the end-all of instruction. We should see programs in the next few years that make DISTAR look as antiquated as the Model-T Ford. DISTAR is simply an attempt to show teachers a better way to teach. Most traditional programs are designed for adults, because adults buy them. Most have never been developed by using kids. When a publisher indicates that the program has been tried out, he usually means that after the program had been completed a supervised tryout was staged for the sole purpose of gathering data that could later be used as promotional information regarding the program. Most instructional programs are copies of other programs. If a new fourth-grade English program has a unit on transformational grammar, within a few years most of the other fourth-grade programs will have the same unit. Whether or not the children can handle the countless units in the program is not a major concern. The salesmen can now be competitive. They can point out that their program has everything that all of the other programs have.

Educational publishing reflects the maxims of traditional education. Just as the traditional educator has no real belief in instruction, the educational publisher typically puts out programs that merely expose children to a variety of topics. He is not restricted by the kind of laws that govern the labels on an aspirin bottle or the construction of a toy. He plays to the naïveté of the material selection committee, which is preoccupied with questions about the illustrations and various other secondary issues that have little to do with whether the program will work in the classroom or whether it can work.

Teachers like Mary need help if they are to discover what teaching is about. Instructional programs are certainly not the complete solution. They can help structure that mysterious process of learning so that Mary can see that what she does affects the performance of her kids. Unfortunately, Mary will not receive the help she needs unless instructional programs receive a far more critical evaluation in terms of their capacity to deliver, and unless educational publishers become accountable for providing material that has a proven potential to teach.

7

The Testing Game

The Standardized Achievement Test

It was spring. Scott was almost eight years old. He had noticed robins, buds on the trees, and green grass in his front yard. Today, Scott was to learn about another sign of spring—the annual spring testing on "standardized achievement tests" (SAT).

Today, Scott was to be a part of the testing ritual. He knew nothing of the energy behind the testing program—the preparations that the teachers made, the last-minute reviews and "polishing" of the children. For Scott it was just a spring day. He recited the pledge to the flag. But the usual reading session did not follow. Instead, his teacher gave the instructions for the Gates-MacGinitie Reading Test published by Teachers' College, Columbia University. This test is one of the more widely used standardized achievement tests. Scott's teacher carefully followed the directions for test administration, cautioning the children not to open the booklets before she told them to do so, and showing them where to print their names. Scott printed his very carefully.

Scott was in the middle reading group of a second-grade classroom. The reading program adopted by Scott's school was a "sight" program, and he generally performed reasonably well for a second-grader: he read falteringly, with some *b* and *d* confusion; he had trouble with the words *and, of, to, for, them, when, the, there, this,* and *that;* sometimes he confused the words *many, very,* and *every;* sometimes he forgot words and had to rely on the picture "cues" to help him figure them out; but of the 850 words that had been presented in the series since Scott's first experience in pre-primers, Scott was fairly consistent on most.

After Scott and his classmates had printed their names, the teacher held up her booklet and pointed to the sample items. "Everyone, point to the first picture on the cover of your booket —right here."

Scott found the picture. It looked like a picture of a store. Next to it were four words.

The teacher explained, "One of these four words goes best with the picture. I will read the words to you. Point to each word as I read it." The teacher read the words, "Sleep . . . only . . . store . . . water. Which word do you think belongs with the picture?"

A number of hands shot up; the teacher called on Nancy Gray. "Store," Nancy said.

"Good. Make a circle around the word *store* on your own booklet. As soon as you have done that, put your pencil down. Do not go ahead."

Mrs. Moore walked around the room and checked every child's work. She then instructed the children to work out the second sample item on the cover of the booklet.

After the children had circled the word for the second item and the teacher had checked their work, she gave those instructions that would become quite familiar to Scott over the next ten years: "As soon as you finish one picture and word, go to the next. Do as many as you can, but don't worry if you don't know all the words. Do the best you can. Any questions? . . . Open your booklets and *begin.*"

Scott noticed that the teacher was holding something that

looked like a watch. He didn't know it was a stopwatch, which would measure precisely the fifteen minutes allotted for the standardized completion of the first part of the test.

Playing the Odds

Scott began. He had received a lot of practice through the worksheets that he did in connection with his reading program. He had learned to first look at the picture, then look at the words, searching for one that might fit the picture. Scott didn't *read* the words, he matched them with the word that he generated by looking at the picture. The first picture was of an apple. Scott looked for a word that looked something like *ap - - -.* He found one and circled it. Scott then looked at the second picture. A paintbrush in a large can. "Can," Scott said to himself and looked for a word that corresponded to *c - -.* There was none. "Brush," Scott said to himself, and tried again. Nothing. "Paint," Scott said to himself. He found two words. No, one of them was not *paint*. It was *p - - - - y*. Scott circled the appropriate word.

That Scott had trouble with some of the items should come as no surprise if you remember that Scott was only a second-grader, not a candidate for a prep school. He had been exposed to 850 words, not 8,500.

The following four items on the Gates-MacGinitie posed obvious problems to Scott (as they would to any second-grader who had not been seriously misgraded by the schools):

> 1. The illustration shows a Christmas tree ornament. The words from which the children are to choose are *settlement, ordinary, innocent,* and *ornament*.
>
> 2. The illustration shows an orchestra. The words from which the children are to choose: *symposium, syndicate, symphony,* and *sycamore*.
>
> 3. The illustration shows a large building. The word choices: *doughnut, dormitory, drawbridge,* and *donation*.

4. The illustration shows a medal. The choices: *medical, medal, model,* and *meddle.*

Scott tried to "remember" some of the words; he scratched his head and squinted from time to time (not because of bad vision but because he hoped to make some of the words look more familiar). When he was working the last item, the teacher told the children in the most standardized way, "Stop writing and put your pencils down."

The test was not over; Scott and his classmates had merely completed the vocabulary section. They now went to the final part of the test, which dealt with "comprehension."

Scott's teacher again went through the sample items with the children. Each item displayed four pictures, below which was a passage. The children were instructed to make a big X on the picture that best illustrated the meaning of the passage or that answered the question in that passage. There were thirty-four items in this part of the test, and the children had fifteen minutes to complete the section. Scott was able to read only three of the thirty-four items without error.

Here are four representative passages from the comprehension section of the test. The italicized words are those that Scott could not read.

1. The nurse is taking a *splinter* out of Betty's foot.

2. Every night at bedtime, she sat with her father in an *armchair* and listened while he read another *chapter* to her.

3. The children were discussing fire *escapes.* Mary said her home was an *apartment building* and the fire *escapes* were *iron* stairs which went up each side of the *building.* Andy said the fire *escapes* in his one-story house were the doors and windows. Mark the building in which Mary lives.

4. *Huge* balloons with baskets under them are *used* by *weathermen.* The baskets carry *instruments* which re-

cord wind speed and *direction, temperature,* and *moisture* high up in the air. The *information* these *instruments* give is *used* to *predict weather* on the ground.
What is used to get *weather information* in the upper
air?

Scott managed to put X's on some of the appropriate pictures, even though he could do little more than guess his way
through the passages. Although Scott was not able to read the
word *splinter* in the first item, only one of the four pictures
shows a nurse doing anything with a girl's foot; Scott was able
to deduce which picture deserved the X. Although Scott could
not read the words *armchair* and *chapter* in the second item, only
one picture showed two people, one of whom was reading. Again
Scott made an X on the appropriate picture. Scott even managed
to X the appropriate picture of the fourth item; he relied primarily on the part of the passage that referred to "balloons with
baskets."

How the Test Results Are Used

When the results of the test were tabulated, Scott's teacher discovered that he had scored above the class average. He had responded correctly on thirty-five of the forty-eight vocabulary
items and on twenty-five of the thirty-four comprehension items.
According to the tables that accompany the test, Scott's reading
score was somewhere in the neighborhood of the beginning-third-
grade level. The average "national norm" score for second-
graders who take the test in May is grade level 2.8. Theoretically,
the average child grows one month in performance for every
month he is in formal instruction, which means that he should
score at grade level 2.8 at this time.

The tests were carefully labeled and filed in the school office.
To make room for the 1973 tests, the 1966 tests, somewhat yel-
lowed, were removed and thrown away. The school psychologist

and resource teacher carefully noted the scores of some newly tested children who were candidates for special classes. The principal and the school psychologist discussed the performance of the school on the tests, agreeing that they might do well to change standardized tests next year. Perhaps unconsciously, both recognized that it is a good idea to change achievement tests every few years so that it is impossible to evaluate whether the teaching in the classroom is improving.

The achievement scores were not used as a basis for diagnosing individual children's problems or to evaluate the effectiveness of the instructional program or the effectiveness of the various teachers. They were not used as a basis for specifying objectives for teacher training, program revisions, or program selections. They were not used as a measure of quality control or as an indicator of specific problems.

Diagnostic Value of the Test

The chances are three to one that in your district the spring testing game is played in full regalia and that the tests are also used in precisely the manner described. Recognize that it is impossible to use these tests in any other way. If we are to make diagnoses about the kind of help that kids need, we must have detailed knowledge about their performance. The very lowest level of information we must have tells us which words the kid can read and which he can't read. Does the standardized test give us this information? Although Scott scored correctly on the vocabulary item that showed the Christmas tree ornament, he couldn't read the word *ornament*. He figured out that one of the words started with the letters *orna*. From this evidence, he concluded that the word was *ornament*. He didn't *read* the word. The actual behavior of reading is not evaluated by the test.

Another feature of the test that further manages to obscure the child's skills is the multiple-choice format. If the child guesses on each item, he would be expected with average luck to get one out of four items correct. A nonreader who took a shot at every item on the comprehension part of the test would be expected to get eight or nine items correct. This performance, according to the tables that accompany the test, would give the child a score of grade level 1.4 (middle-first-grade level). This makes it all but impossible to assert how much the child knows as compared to how lucky he is. A second-grader who scores close to grade level may be virtually a nonreader but a good guesser. At the other extreme would be the second-grader who reads very well but who reads all of the words to see which fits the picture most accurately. On most of the items, he isn't able to read all of the words and skips the item. He is penalized for lack of behavior that has very little to do with actual reading—guessing.

Another problem with the test has to do with the convention of expressing the child's performance as a *number*, called score. These often manage to conceal absurdities in the child's performance. Scott managed to get the weather-balloon item correct. However, he missed items that were far easier. Could anybody seriously entertain the idea that he failed to read the easier items and managed to read the more difficult item?

The most questionable aspect of the test is the apparent lack of relationship between what has been taught the children and the material presented in the test. It is improbable that second-grade children have encountered words like *predict, apartment, moisture, discussing,* etc. Yet these words appear on the test, which would indicate that the test is not testing what was supposed to have been taught—it is merely testing "reading" of some sort, which makes the results of questionable value. Perhaps the best way to demonstrate the relative uselessness of the test is to give Scott's test to a knowledgeable teacher and tell her to "analyze" Scott's performance by making consistent statements about Scott's reading ability. The analyst, noting Scott's performance on the weather-balloon item, would be forced to conclude that if Scott actually read and understood this item, he could perform far in excess of the second- or third-grade level.

She would be faced with the basic problem, however, of trying to decide whether Scott actually read and understood the item. Does she know that he wasn't guessing or cueing from a few words? And if it is possible that Scott did not actually read and understand the item, can she determine precisely how he went about handling it? Then she has to reconcile his performance on this item with that on some of the easier items. Since the test gives her no information about Scott's actual reading behavior, she can do little more than speculate.

The "Normal-Distribution" Curve

Conclusion: The standardized test does not provide information that is sufficiently detailed or accurate to provide information about what to teach a child. The goal is, rather, to document that children follow a natural pattern of growth. The achievement tests are designed to produce a bell-shaped curve of distribution. Using the premise that there must be a curve that describes achievement, the test designers construct a test that spreads the distribution of children. Thus the designers include items like the one about the weather balloon. Often the standardized achievement test is "timed," to further spread the distribution. When a rate criterion is introduced, individual differences become even more exaggerated.

Although school administrators have great confidence in the standardized tests and spend a great deal of money on such testing, they don't seem to understand the obvious limitations of the test or the principles of norms that dictate the construction of the tests. In some New York City schools (where the Metropolitan Achievement Test is used), the administrators give the second-grade children the first-grade test, reasoning that the children will have a greater opportunity to succeed on the "easier" test. For a child to score at grade level on the first-grade test administered in May, however, the child would have to correctly score seventy-three to seventy-seven items. If a solid reader misinterpreted several items, didn't understand what a couple of pictures illustrated, or became confronted with words that he didn't know, he would score below grade level. (If he misses more than four items, he scores below grade level.) If the same child correctly responded to slightly more than half of the items on the second-grade achievement test, however, he would score at grade level.

Criterion-referenced Tests

In 1964, a new term, "criterion-referenced tests," was introduced into educational literature by Robert Glaser. While the traditional test is concerned with the "norm," the criterion-referenced test is concerned with the *objectives of instruction,* and is based on the idea that a school district selected particular instructional programs.

The criterion-referenced test says in effect, "So the instructional program promises to deliver each skill. Let's test and see whether the children were taught, after each of the exercises has been completed." The items in the test are those items that the instructional program supposedly taught. Important skills are tested. If a skill is not taught in the program, it is not tested. If the children score 100 percent on the test, we don't have to revise the test to demonstrate that these children are different, we know that they are. In addition we know that all have been taught the skills laid out in a particular instructional program.

The criterion-referenced test is an integral part of a school system that focuses on quality control. Here is how it can be used.

How to Use the Test

First, the district would construct a test based on the fundamental ground rule that the author of the instructional program must be tested. He may suggest that certain readiness exercises lead to performance on actual reading tasks. Test him. He may suggest that the exercises outlined in the teacher's guide teach children how to discuss and comprehend a story. Test him. The idea is not to impose *your* ideas of how to teach reading and not to construct a series of "necessary steps" that a child must take in order to read.

By constructing items that test each of the instructional steps in the program, we construct a test that is capable of evaluating the progress of the children from exercise to exercise in the program.

Next, the district would administer the test to a controlled cadre of perhaps a dozen teachers who would follow the teacher's guide for the program to the letter, or as closely as possible. They would receive training and practice in performing according to the teacher's guide. They would not go beyond the manual and the reading exercises; they would not improvise except according to the directions of the program. The purpose of the cadre is to determine *how effectively the program performs when the teachers are following that program as closely as possible.*

After the cadre has been trained, the district evaluates the performance of the children taught by these teachers. By testing the children every two weeks to evaluate the children's performance in mastering each of the skills in the program, the administration would be in a position to pinpoint activities within the program that are poorly designed and are not capable of fulfilling the implicit promises of the program.

In addition, the administration would test all children who are going through the program in the district. Most of the children would not be taught by cadre teachers. The criterion-referenced test would show discrepancies between the performance of the cadre and that of the other teachers (since the other teachers would probably not be following the program as closely as the cadre would). Pinpointing these discrepancies would help the administration to identify teacher-training problems and perhaps solutions to some of the problems that the cadre encountered when following the author's instructions for teaching. Let's say that a particular skill was mastered by ninety-two percent of the children taught by cadre teachers but by only forty-eight percent of the children taught by teachers at large. This information would tell us that the skill is perfectly teachable if the teacher follows the program. The low performance of the teachers at large indicates that they are simply not following the program. To correct this situation the administration would take two steps. First, it would provide training to ensure that the teachers were capable of executing the exercises in the way called for by the program. Second, it would monitor teachers to document that they were following the program.

Discovering Better Teaching Models

Let's say that one skill was mastered by only sixty percent of the cadre-taught children and fifty-four percent of the children taught by teachers at large. Obviously, a revision of the program is implied. The district must make up some new exercises and add some exercises that will allow at least ninety percent of the children to master the skill (assuming that the skill is important). By examining the results of each teacher at large, the administration would probably discover that some teachers are teaching eighty or ninety percent of their children this skill. They are not following the program, but what they do works better than the exercises in the program. The activities that these teachers use could serve as prototypes for constructing new and effective exercises.

The criterion-referenced test can also be used to make diagnostic statements about individual children. We can identify those children who are consistently not being taught skills or who are misplaced in the program. Furthermore, we can specify the skills they have not been taught.

Information Needed for Intelligent Decisions

The next task facing the district is to make an intelligent decision about whether the program it uses should be revised so that each of the activities teaches at least ninety percent of the children and whether the teachers should be trained in presenting those exercises in which the teachers at large fall down. If the program revisions are too extensive and the amount of training too great, the district may decide to scrap the program in favor of one that is capable of delivering on more of the exercises. To make this decision, the district needs the kind of information that comes from a criterion-referenced test that is administered at least four or five times throughout the year. There are probably less than four school districts in the United States that follow anything approximating the criterion-referenced procedure outlined here. Yet all districts—hundreds of them—make decisions about purchasing instructional programs. Some states (California, Texas, and others) adopt instructional programs for their entire state. Programs are purchased, installed, and used with no knowledge of the program's effectiveness, of the specific sections of the program that should be revised (or made more articulate), or of the specific training requirements that must be implemented if the program is to teach the children.

Why Not Use Criterion-referenced Measures?

School administrators offer two other arguments for not using criterion-referenced tests of instruction:

1. They argue that the criterion-referenced measure does not indicate how each child performs in relationship to a "national norm." These norms are usually not current. Rather, they were established before the test was published (or revised), and the

norm against which children are compared today may be five years old or older. Also, the procedures used for establishing these norms are sometimes questionable. The authors of one of the more widely used achievement tests carefully screened all "poor" children from the norming population. Only middle-class and upper-class children were represented in the sample. The elimination of the poor children makes for a very high norm. The authors of another achievement test asked administrators in different districts to allow them to administer the test at "typical schools." One doesn't have to know much about the psychology of administrators to surmise that they nominated not average schools but their best schools, so that they could say in mock modesty, "Well, we have a very good district, you know."

2. The administrators argue that there is a difference between diagnostic, evaluative, and normative tests. They contend that the criterion-referenced test is diagnostic. It does not satisfy the needs for evaluation and for comparing children who are placed in different instructional programs. In one sense, this objection is valid. If two children in different programs are given only criterion-referenced tests, they may not receive any common test items and it is therefore difficult to make statements about the comparative effectiveness of each program. If the two children receive the same test, however, we can say which program is doing a better job. Although the administrator's objection is valid, the traditional achievement test is not the answer. One of the implicit promises of a reading program is that it will teach children to read. At the end of the year, the children should be able to read the first part of the textbooks that they will read during the following year. Let's say that we selected a couple of short paragraphs from the third-grade science text and social-science text. All children, regardless of which second-grade reading program they went through, would be tested on these paragraphs. All would read the selected passages orally. All would answer questions based on these passages. By using this type of test we could make very strong comparative statements about various programs. The test would be "standardized," in that all

children would receive the same test. The test would actually sample the behavior in which we're interested.

The administrator's objection that criterion-referenced tests are merely diagnostic is wrong because they can do anything that the traditional test does and do it better. They can be used to compare the children who are in the second grade this year with the performance of second-graders last year. They can show overall improvement and changes in each of the various skills taught in the program.

The reason that criterion-referenced tests can do much more than traditional standardized tests is that they provide more detailed information. If we are told that there is an animal on a farm, we don't know what kind of animal the statement refers to. Possibly it is a horse, a cow, a goat, or even an elephant. A statement about a spotted pig with a knick in his right ear and a blue mark on the end of his nose gives us the specific information for identifying the animal in question. This statement also gives us all of the information that the first statement gave—that an animal is on the farm. In the same way, the criterion-referenced test gives more information than is provided by the categories "vocabulary" and "comprehension." The test indicates specifically the kind of vocabulary on which the child is weak. It indicates which of the comprehension activities taught in the program have succeeded with each child and which have not. The test allows us to make statements about such broad categories as "comprehension," and at the same time allows us to look at the various exercises that comprise "comprehension." This detailed information serves as a basis for evaluating programs and comparing the performance of children from year to year.

Traditional Instruction in New Trappings

During the past two or three years, criterion-referenced material has become topical in the schools. Systems such as the Wisconsin Design for Reading Skill Development and the Westinghouse

Learning Corporation offer "criterion-referenced systems." These systems violate the notion of true criterion-referenced testing in an important way: they imply specific teaching that may not be in the program.

Here is an item from the Westinghouse Learning Corporation:

> The teacher says: "Read the story about Ed and the dog to yourselves. [Pause. You may help individual students with unfamiliar words.] Have you all finished? Look at the groups of words below the story. Now cover the story with your hand. Find the group of words that tells *where* Ed saw the dog, and darken the space below it."

The behavior is the same old behavior tested on the standardized achievement test. There are four spaces below the passage. And the passage is the same old kind of passage. The only difference between this item and the old type that appears on a standardized achievement test is that this item has an objective. The problem created by the item is that it implies teaching if we are to be assured that all children will respond to the instructions. The item is therefore not merely testing what had been taught in the instructional program; it implies additional teaching.

The Curve Is Still With Us

The school's addiction to norms is not limited to standardized tests. Even in college, professors proudly assert that they grade "on the curve." If the class were composed of kids who thoroughly mastered every skill taught, only a few would receive A's. The others would be relegated to a lesser position on the bell-shaped curve. Teachers in the elementary school who have reputations of being "tough" brag that they give only a few A's each year.

The basic assumption from which these teachers operate is that most children are normal and only a very few have the exceptional qualities necessary for a top performance.

Something is seriously wrong with this formula. A second-grade teacher who gives only two or three A's either has unrealistic standards or is a rotten teacher, capable of teaching only two or three of her thirty students to an acceptable level of performance.

Grades obviously must be based on some sort of standard. This standard should not be expressed in terms of the child's effort or his goodwill. (What if a particular kid scores above the norm in a classroom in which no children read?) Nor should it be expressed in terms of a "norm." It should be expressed in terms of the skills the child has achieved and should reflect the progress the school has made with the child during the grading period. This is not to say that all children come to school with the same skills or that all of them progress at the same rate. But certain minimum standards must be met with even those children who are "immature," "unready," or just plain "slow." By the end of the first-grade year, for example, all children should have mastered basic reading skills. Some children will have progressed far beyond the basics, but the standard that we must have for all children is that they will receive the *minimum* teaching—that amount necessary to teach them simple decoding and comprehension. Every child who attends school regularly should achieve this level of competence. To the parent the grade should be an indication of the degree to which the school has met this requirement.

Criterion-referenced tests allow the district to make accurate and meaningful statements about the progress of each child. An ideal report card would be a "flow chart" showing the various skills taught for a particular grade. The teacher would indicate by coloring in appropriate lines how many lessons the child has mastered during a particular grading period. The difference between this kind of report card and the traditional one is that traditional reporting is based on the assumption that the child who receives a C has mastered seventy-five percent of everything that has been taught (with all skills taught simultaneously to all children). The criterion-referenced report indicates those skills the child has mastered to a criterion of nearly 100 percent. The child's first report card can be used as a basis for showing how much that child improves as he progresses through the school. Let's say that he masters only thirty lessons in reading during the first grading period. His initial rate is thirty lessons per grading period. If he masters forty lessons during the second or third grading period (which he will do if the instruction is careful), we can show that the child is not only learning skills to nearly a 100 percent criterion of performance but improving and learning at a faster rate.

Some parents are understandably puzzled when they are initially introduced to the reporting system based on the criterion-referenced tests; however, once they understand that it provides them with detailed information about what their child is being taught, they come to respect it as a report by the school on the school's effectiveness in working with their child.

The Need for Standards

Recently a number of eloquent pleas have suggested doing away with grading systems and standards in the schools. Prompted by frustration over the failure of minority children in traditional schools, liberals have argued how wrong we are to impose our middle-class values on such groups as urban blacks, pointing out that our standards are not relevant to these children. The liberals attack standardized tests, grading systems within the school, and any mechanism that would provide a comparison of children from different backgrounds. These liberals are either very myopic or supreme racists. We must have absolute standards in the schools and we must see to it that all children are taught to the same standard of excellence. Our job is not to compromise the standards and in so doing rob the minority children of the opportunity for equal education or equal competence; our job is to map the road with the clarity and the technical detail that will render the road more than a limited-access freeway for those who come from advantaged backgrounds.

I'm sure that the liberals who suggest that there should be different standards for different ethnic groups don't realize that they are setting the stage for continued racial prejudice. On one hand they argue that minority children have a great deal to offer; on the other, they seem quite doubtful that these children can succeed. And they seem to overlook the question, Who will suffer from the adoption of different standards for different groups? Certainly not the advantaged child. The standards are already higher for him. Furthermore, he may attend a private school. We already have low standards for poor children. New York City and other urban centers are dotted with living documentation of the different standards used for black, Puerto Rican, and Mexican children. In some Brooklyn junior high schools, only four percent of the children perform at grade level on standardized tests. The tests may be unreasonable, but they are not so insensitive that they can't show the incredible standard that we currently have for these children.

Picture a high school in which three out of four children cannot read on a beginning-third-grade level. Such high schools exist. They are monuments to the "different" standard we currently have for some children. If we close our eyes to these problems, arguing that those children perform the way they do because they are different and should be measured by a different standard, we will justify the situation that currently exists and we will license the continuation of these abuses. The parents of most poor kids know the game. They realize that education is the only vehicle that will transport their children from the slums. Their children must be educated in the same competencies as the middle-class child. Perhaps the sequence and format of instruction will differ, but the end result must be the same.

One of the major jobs facing us is to caution the liberals about the implications of their racist arguments. They must have some faith that black kids, red kids, and brown kids can make it by the same standard. To make sure that they make it, we must examine the way we test and the way we teach all our children. We must replace traditional standardized tests with instruments that are capable of measuring the effectiveness of instruction. Then we must see to it that the tests are used to guarantee effective instruction for all kids.

8

A Kid's Rights Under the Law

The Right to a Quality Education

Today, education is perhaps the most important function of state and local governments. Compulsory school attendance laws and the great expenditures for education both demonstrate our recognition of the importance of education to our democratic society. It is required in the performance of our most basic public responsibilities, even service in the armed forces. It is the very foundation of good citizenship. Today it is a principal instrument in awakening the child to cultural values, in preparing him for later professional training, and in helping him to adjust normally in his environment. In these days, it is doubtful that any child may reasonably be expected to succeed in life if he is denied the opportunity of an education. Such an opportunity, where the state has undertaken to provide it, is a right which must be made available to all on equal terms.

The gentlemen who wrote that statement were justices of the United States Supreme Court. The quotation comes from their 1954 decision on desegregation. Although the decision centered around segregation within the schools, the Court argued on *the importance of an education*. It refers to the child's right, made available to all on equal terms. Although the intent of the statement seems clear, even to the degree of implying a *constitutional* right to the kind of education that would allow him to "succeed in life," the question of the child's rights is quite complicated. It has been analyzed in different law-review articles and has been the subject of controversy both in the courts and in educational circles.

The 1954 case seemed to set the stage for cases brought against school districts on the grounds that the district violated the Fourteenth Amendment, which provides for equal protection under the law. According to the 1954 decision, facilities that are separate cannot be equal.

Educational Malpractice

Based on the apparent implications of the 1954 case, desegregation orders were issued to various states, some state laws were held to be unconstitutional and in violation of a person's right to equal protection, and the federal courts heard cases that seemed to go beyond the issues of segregation and to further question the rights of the children. Also, some concerned educators developed arguments that seemed perhaps to be consistent with the intent of the Supreme Court's stands on equality. Don Stewart wrote a fascinating book, *Educational Malpractice, the Big Gamble in Our Schools*. Stewart's central argument is that teachers have long insisted that they are professionals. He then points out that if they are professionals they are possibly guilty of malpractice, legally defined as follows:

> Malpractice is dereliction from professional duty, whether intentional, criminal, or merely negligent, by one rendering professional services that result in injury,

loss or damage to the recipient of those services or to those entitled to rely upon them or that affects the public interests adversely.

In Stewart's hypothetical educational-malpractice suit, the parents of a high-school dropout are suing for $35,000 damages, which the student will lose as a result of not being able to complete his high-school education. The following excerpt from Stewart's book is taken from that trial. One of the tenth-grade teachers who flunked the kid is on the stand:

STUDENT ATTORNEY: As a teacher, are you concerned about learning?

TEACHER: (Almost every teacher would answer, "Yes," to this question.)

STUDENT ATTORNEY: As a representative of your school district, do you believe that your administrators and school board are concerned about learning?

TEACHER: (In most situations, the teacher would answer, "Yes," to this question.)

STUDENT ATTORNEY: [To the judge and jury] I would like to enter as Exhibit 1 the transcript of this student in which it says in black and white that during a test given in the ninth grade, this student was found to be able to read only at the fifth-grade level. I would also like to enter Exhibits 2, 3, 4, and 5, the textbooks that were given to the student when he entered tenth grade, and also Exhibits 6, 7, 8, and 9, which are sworn statements by experts that each of

these textbooks was written at
a tenth-grade or higher reading
level. [To teacher on witness
stand:] As a teacher interested
in learning and as a representative of a school district interested
in learning, does it make sense
to give a student who you know
reads at fifth- or maybe sixth-
grade level, instructional materials which are written at tenth-
grade level or higher?

Stewart's perception of the problem is penetrating, and his
arguments seem strong. If the system is supposed to *educate* all
children and if the system has professional responsibility for such
education, then the system is clearly accountable for the performance of kids and may be found guilty of malpractice charges.

No Obligation to Educate

However, these ifs are big ones, and they are not affirmed either
by laws or by the federal courts' decisions regarding the consti-
tutionality of the state laws. The law does not view teachers as
professionals, in any ordinary sense of the word. The problem is
a double one. The state laws are not sufficiently clear about what
an education is or what kind of performance the state is accountable to provide. All states have compulsory school attendance.
Yet there are few statements that relate to what the state is
obliged to do with respect to changing the behavior of the children. According to the California Education Code, California's
policy is to "provide an educational opportunity to every individual to the end that every student leaving school should be prepared to enter the world of work." Yet in the case of an autistic
child who had not benefited from the instruction provided by the

state, the Supreme Court held that the schools are obliged to provide instruction of "suitable capacity," which, according to the Court, means "the ability of the child to acquire at least basic vocabulary, reading, writing and mathematical skills commensurate with lower grammar school levels and the ability of the child to participate individually as a pupil and contributing [sic] to his classroom group."

This description is clearly after-the-fact and circular. A child demonstrates at the end of his formal education that he performs according to the minimum standards for those who are to be provided "education," and the state is able to maintain that it in fact educated a borderline child. If the child falls below this level, regardless of the kind of "instruction" provided, the state can blame the child, and discharge him, with the sanction of the courts.

The Lau Case

Another California case that reached the Supreme Court, *Lau v. Nichols*, did not help to clarify rights of children. The case involved Chinese-speaking children in San Francisco who were not being provided instruction in English. Although these children received no instruction in English, some Chinese-speaking children in the district were receiving such instruction. The appellate court held against Lau, declaring, "The needs of the citizen must be reconciled with the finite resources available to meet those needs." Paul Gordon, in a *University of San Francisco Law Review* article, commented, "It is a travesty that a school system which denies thousands of children an education because of the unavailability of funding, continues to squander its budget on classes in which the children cannot understand the language of instruction."

The case was reversed by the U.S. Supreme Court on the basis of the Civil Rights Act of 1964, which bans discrimination based "on the grounds of race, color, or national origin" in "any program or activity receiving federal financial assistance." In his opinion, Justice Douglas made some statements implying that the schools had professional responsibility for the performance of children. After pointing out that English is the basic language of instruction for all schools in California, Justice Douglas observed, "Basic English skills are at the very core of what these public schools teach. Imposition of a requirement that before a child can effectively participate in the educational program, he must already have acquired those basic skills is to make a mockery of public education." The *Lau* decision, however, leaves the right of the child unclear and the obligation of the schools even less clear.

Babysitting Responsibility of Schools

The California case of *David P.* has received a great deal of publicity. The suit stems from the fact that although David was promoted from grade to grade with no indication from his teachers that he had problems, his poor academic performance prevented him from graduating and seriously reduced the number of choices that he will have as a working adult. The argument offered by his legal counsel is that he has received no form of education. His counsel contends that since educationally handicapped children are described by the California Education Code as persons who "cannot benefit from the regular educational programs," they do not receive an education—by definition—unless a special program of instruction is provided, because by definition they *cannot* benefit from a regular educational program. No special program was provided for David. Therefore, he received *no* benefits. The question is not one of degree, but of absolute deprivation. This point is extremely important, although there is no certainty that David will win his case.

At least two cases have held that the schools do have an obligation to educate all children. These cases have dealt with handicapped children who had been excluded from public schools. The Pennsylvania Association for Retarded Children sued the state for not providing all children with publicly supported education. The court held that the state had denied the children's right to education. In a similar case, Mills brought charges against the Board of Education of the District of Columbia. Judge Skelly Wright held that a constitutional right to education existed for all children regardless of handicapping conditions. (The Pennsylvania case dealt with retarded children, while the decision in the Mills case had implications for *all* handicapped children.)

The Rodriguez Case—a Big Setback

After the 1972 *Mills* decision, it seemed as if there was a real possibility that the right to an education would be applied to the discriminatory practices that result in schools where children are not taught. However, a case of great significance was heard before the United States Supreme Court in 1973. The plaintiffs in *San Antonio Independent School District v. Rodriguez* charged that the Texas system of school financing produced inequality of educational access for the poor. School financing was based on the revenue collected through property tax. The inner-city school district generated only twenty-six dollars in tax for each pupil, while a different tax base in other districts yielded $333 per pupil. The contention was that this practice of school financing discriminated against the poor.

The court, however, held that (a) there was no violation of a constitutional right (since the "right" to education is neither explicitly nor implicitly a constitutional right); (b) the "discrimination" against the poor is permissible because the poor are not *totally deprived* of an education; rather, they are "receiving a poorer quality of education."

The children in the Rodriguez case did not choose to have a "poorer quality of education." Clearly it was imposed on them in what seems to be a discriminatory manner. How, then, is it possible to reconcile the fact that equal libraries that are "separate" are construed as a violation of constitutional rights, while the more flagrant violation of "equal educational opportunity" in the Rodriguez case is considered permissible?

The answer is that the *Rodriguez* decision cannot be reconciled with the 1954 decision, regardless of the amount of legal contortions one goes through. As Justice Marshall and Justice Douglas said in their dissent, "The Majority's holding can only be seen as a retreat from our historic commitment to equality of educational opportunity and as unsupportable acquiescence in a system which deprives children in their earliest years of the chance to reach their full potential as citizens."

At first blush, it seems that the Nixon Court has made it impossible for you to protect yourself against incompetence in the schools and against mere teaching motions that have little to do with the performance of the kids. It leaves the average parent in an awkward position. According to state legislation, the child must attend school. Yet the schools and the teachers are apparently not accountable for more than keeping the window shades level, being physically present in the classroom, and perhaps following the prescribed syllabus of study (even though there are rarely provisions to check on whether the teacher actually does).

Identifying a Suspect Class

By digging a little deeper into the various court cases, however, we find that some vestiges of hope remain.

For this excursion we have to look at some of the legal considerations involved in federal court decisions. There are several ways to present a case of unequal protection under the law. One tactic is to show that a constitutional right has been violated by a particular law or practice. The Rodriguez case rules out the possibility of education being considered a constitutional or "fundamental" right. Another tactic, somewhat more complicated, is to establish a case that would involve a suspect class, which is a clearly identifiable group with a disability that has experienced a history of discrimination and is relatively powerless. To date, the only suspect classes that have been identified are those that involve racial-ethnic groups (which in itself seems somewhat discriminatory). To establish a class as suspect, the lawyer has to show that the group can be identified in a fairly precise way, that it has been the object of discrimination, and that it is politically powerless.

There is a good case for showing that mentally retarded and perhaps other groups of "labeled" handicapped children satisfy the criteria of a suspect class. Mental retardation is a disability that can be identified; it carries with it a stigma of inferiority which results in different forms of discrimination; and the retarded have received judicial protection, an indication of political powerlessness.

In other words, if your child is mentally retarded or has some other label that relates to an identifiable disability, the chances are that he is eligible for equal protection under the law, which means that the state is obliged to provide an education that is suited to his needs. Translated into actual practice, this means that your child is often eligible for at least some form of custodial care, perhaps without much attention to education. As long as the formal facilities are provided, the state can claim that your child is protected equally under the law. (The *Mills* decision noted above carried the education several steps further by scrutinizing the qualification of the teachers, the curriculum, and other aspects of the program planned for the handicapped. However, nearly all of the other decisions that involve "labeled" children have been limited to making the school program available to the child, with no stipulation about the quality of the program.)

The School Failure

Where does all this leave the school failure, the child whose failure is created by the schools? He may live in a state that takes a more lenient view of the child's right to an education. The various states do not have to reject the child's right to an education merely because the U.S. Supreme Court does not recognize this right as a constitutional right. If the school failure is so fortunate, it would be possible to bring suit against the state on the simple grounds that his right to an education has been denied. Also, the state may not require absolute deprivation as a standard for determining whether there has been a violation. The state court might be visionary enough to recognize that reading at the fourth-grade level in the twelfth grade is not good enough. On the other hand, the state may follow the lead of the Nixon Court and treat the child's plight with the same consideration that the poor kids in San Antonio received.

It may be possible, however, to construct a case that would establish the school failure as a suspect class, in which case constitutional rulings could be applied to state practices. The first step is to show that the school failure has an immutable trait or disability. There should be no serious problem here. In fact, those very achievement tests and grade-level standards that are used in the schools can be used as instruments to document the "disability" or trait shared by the school failure.

The next step is to show that there is purposeful or systematic discrimination directed against the school failure. It shouldn't be too difficult to show that teachers like these children less, treat them with less respect and far less reinforcement, more frequently give them assignments that they are incapable of handling, and exclude them from a variety of activities that are available to the school success. The school failure is particularly discriminated against in terms of the skills that he is taught. Often he is not taught important language skills or arithmetic skills, merely because he can't read. The final step is to show that he is politically powerless. The question would actually be one of *relative* political powerlessness, since no children have the political power of adults. It should be possible to show that even as an adult the school failure is as politically powerless as the average black or Mexican American.

Assuming that it would be possible to show that the school failure is a suspect class, the next hurdle, and the most critical one, would be to show that the school failure has been totally deprived of educational services.

What Benefit for the School Failure?

According to the *Rodriguez* decision, the plaintiffs' case "might arguably [have met] the criteria established in . . . prior cases" if a suspect class had been established and if the children experienced total deprivation of the desired benefits. Obviously, we can't show that the school failure has been excluded from the classroom. We can't argue that he has been denied the benefit of sitting in that classroom just as the other kids sit. However, it may be possible for us to borrow a tactic used in the *David P.* case, which is to show that the failure child is educationally handicapped. According to the state educational code's definition, the educationally handicapped may be one who "cannot benefit from regular educational programs." If such a definition is used, then the school failure is incapable of benefiting from the regular program. Therefore, he has been absolutely deprived of the benefits.

Another way to establish the absolute-deprivation requirement may be to show that although educational benefits are supposed to be provided through the school, there is no indication that the school failure received any actual benefits. This could be achieved by reading the goals or purpose of the educational program, as contained in the state educational code, and comparing the description of the supposed benefits with the actual empirical data on the school failure's performance. Not only would this procedure show the absolute deprivation of benefits received by the school failure; it would document that in fact the district has provided the school failure with "services" that are contrary to the established goals of the educational program. The failure is not adequately prepared for the world of work. He doesn't have the attitudes of "citizenship" that sometimes are noted in the educational code, nor does he have the competencies that are implied in descriptions of the academic programs that are offered.

Who Creates the School Failure?

To ensure that the case would have a potentially productive purpose in prompting changes in the school, we would want to make it clear that the school failure is created by the schools. If we don't take this step, we won't be able to make any progress in establishing accountability procedures for the school that amount to more than motions. The idea is not merely to make programs available to children; the idea is to make *programs that work* available. Therefore, we have to show that (1) different teachers create school failures at different but predictable rates; (2) the school has established insufficient (and in many cases no) provisions for training, monitoring, or removing teachers who produce school failures at an unreasonable rate; and (3) the schools are negligent because they are not even cognizant of the rate at which different teachers produce failure.

We could ideally make these points by comparing, for example, the performance of the best first-grade teacher in the district (with respect to kid performance) with the worst teacher. For the sake of argument, let's say that the two teachers worked with the same range of children and that all the children were reasonably "ready," as measured by the school's readiness instruments that are supposed to judge the child's readiness. Let's say that the first teacher consistently produced .4 failures a year (which means that less than one child from the class each year failed to master basic skills), while the other teacher produced failures at the rate of six per year. We could probably demonstrate that the school system was unaware of this consistent difference. It would probably be possible to further establish that the schools have made no real attempt to change the performance of the teacher who consistently creates an unreasonable number of failures. For example, we could show that none of the supervisory staff in the district has ever demonstrated the ability to teach at a low failure rate, that the school does not use low failure rate as a criterion for selecting people to "supervise," and that the supervisors aren't provided with a schedule that will allow them to actually train teachers.

Due Process

The major argument that the state would probably use to justify the current structure of the system is that to change procedures would be expensive. The counterargument would be to show that the school failure is indeed expensive for a number of reasons. Not only are his capabilities as a citizen reduced by failure to receive an actual education that prepared him for the world of work, but also the amount of effort needed to change his behavior once he becomes an established failure is substantially increased. To implement a remedy of patching up an older kid who has been mistaught reading requires far more time and money than is needed to teach him properly the first time. If the school is not prepared to acknowledge responsibility for these kids, then the school is not actually prepared to provide educational services.

If the school acknowledges its responsibility under the educational code but argues that it is not financially feasible to implement procedures needed to guard against failure, the school is admitting that it is arbitrarily incarcerating some children and it is doing so without following the established procedures of due process. In this situation, the state law requiring mandatory attendance in the schools would seem to violate the rights of the children. The school would be knowingly committing some children to a program of failure (not education) without giving the child notice, or without establishing a hearing at which the child would have a chance to defend himself against this arbitrary discriminatory practice.

Stimulating School Reform

One point must be made clear about the litigation tactics described above. The purpose of a suit is not to punish the school or the teachers; it is not to vent vindictiveness or play the empty game of seeing which of the "cherished" beliefs we can tumble next. The suit would have the purpose of stimulating changes in the school that would in turn affect teachers' colleges and educational publishing, and would focus the school administration's emphasis on the classroom, not on the peripheral aspects of the schools. A reform is needed if our cities are to remain more than a place of residence for dummies and misfits. The United States probably has three resources that are still unmatched by any other country: agriculture, inventiveness, and our kids. We spend a great deal of money on education. The purpose of the suit would be to protect our investment by providing the best possible educational benefits for these kids.

The description I provided of the suit is slightly simplified. (For example, there are tests in addition to the test of strict scrutiny that may be used by the court.) However, let's assume that a court ruled in favor of the plaintiff. The case would imply that the schools are responsible for the school failure (or at least for a specified, reasonable percentage of failure). Some great inequities would be created. In some instances, teachers who are no more at fault for their failure than Mary is would be "blamed" and branded as child abusers. Some school programs would be labeled as failure programs even though the school has actually done the best it can to avoid failure and to provide the children with a good program. Several years ago, we worked on a performance contract basis with a school district and provided a program that was not successful. We tried; the school district cooperated; yet in the available time we were not able to change the behavior of the teachers or the children by any significant degree. On the other hand, we did fail and it is certainly not the children's fault that we did. We should not be excused for our failure any more than somebody else should be.

Although such inequities will result, when we weigh these against the inequities that currently exist we see that they are slight. There are currently bilingual programs for foreign-speaking children that produce no measurable results. There are programs in the junior high schools and high schools that result in a steady drop in performance. (For example, the high-school SAT scores have dropped each year for the past five years.) A real reform is needed, not merely a new vocabulary. Rather, the procedures that are currently spawning failure in the school must stop. The results of quasi-permissiveness are evident in the family and in the school. But change will not occur from within. The schools are no more capable of consistent, uniform change than the oil industry and the automobile industry are. Large groups that have a large investment in established procedures become autonomous organizations that seem to be guided not by the will and direction of the "leaders" within the group, but rather by the inertia and the sheer weight of tradition. Often a crisis is needed to stimulate such change. Each day that we delay bringing that crisis about is another day in the unconscionable incarceration of hundreds of thousands of kids like Jimmy and Andy.

New Laws Are Needed

Historically, laws—like sand dunes—have changed under the winds of social forces. They have been buffeted by fear, reaction, hope, and honest concern. They have emerged and multiplied from the turn of a word. The Federal Bureau of Investigation and much federal legislation sprang from a few words about interstate commerce in the Constitution. Simple statements in state constitutions about educating children have given birth to tedious codes and legislation relating to the financing, operation, and responsibilities of the school.

The laws relating to the training and certification of teachers, responsibilities of the schools, and educational publishing are perfectly inadequate to establish or sustain education either as a viable service for all kids or as an honest profession for those engaged in it. The courts are currently faced with the problems of working from existing laws and trying to find remedies that are equitable. The problem, however, is primarily not a judicial but a legislative one. New laws must appear. But in order for them to be born, a strong social force must exist, and that force must be strong enough to withstand great pressure exerted by those who have a strong investment in things the way they are.

9

How to Deal with the Schools

Before setting a course for bringing about change in the school, we have to address ourselves to two questions:

(1) What kind of plan would provide for the systematic protection of the children's rights?

(2) How does a parent, a teacher, or an administrator go about taking steps that will help the school district move in the appropriate direction?

Let's begin with an ideal plan for the schools. In an ideal system, all teachers and aides would have contracts that specified their teaching responsibilities and clearly outlined the causes for dismissal, which would be:

1. Failing to attend in-service meetings or to perform adequately on in-service assignments;
2. Failing on two occasions (which are documented by the principal) to carry out assignments given by the supervisor;
3. Failing to achieve minimum performance requirements for the children by the end of the year.

The contract would further indicate the terms of "probation and promotion."

The Quota System

In a workable system, all new teachers would receive *daily* training, the type Linda received. Also, they would be assigned classes of gifted or high-IQ children. These children require the least presentation skills. Although the teaching-performance "quota" for these children is higher than it is for average or disadvantaged children, the children begin at a point that is higher than that of the average child; they are familiar with instruction; therefore they can proceed at a healthy rate. In most cases, the teacher will not need the precise presentation and correction skills that are demanded by successful work with the lower-performing children. Several studies have demonstrated that virtually *any* program works with high-IQ children. As we move down to the average child, fewer programs are effective. When we go to the slower children—the disadvantaged and the retarded —very few programs work. This fact merely points out that the high-IQ children have skills that compensate for many possible faults in the teacher's presentation. The system would have safeguards to ensure that these children do not receive slipshod instruction. If the new teacher does not meet her performance objectives with high-IQ children during the first four months of school (as indicated by the criterion-referenced tests), she is placed on extended probation, is relieved of primary teaching responsibility for the children, and becomes a "trainee." At the end of the year, a decision is made about whether she should be reinstated and given another four-month probationary test as a teacher.

Teachers who meet their objectives with the gifted or relatively high-IQ children during their first year are given the choice of remaining with the high-IQ children or moving to the "average children."

If a second-year teacher meets or surpasses "quota" with average kids, she is again given a choice. She may either continue to work with the average children or work with the third classification of children, the high-risk children. If the teacher has performed successfully with the children who are easier to teach and those who are moderately difficult, her chances of success with the high-risk children are very good. If she decides to work with the high-risk children, she will be placed on a four-month probation. At the end of this period she will be returned to working with the average children if she is not meeting quota.

Since the greatest skill is required to teach the high-risk children, teachers of these children would receive the highest base salary. Their base would be one fifth above the base for average children. Teachers of the high-IQ children (the easiest to teach) receive a base salary that is one fifth less than that of the teacher of average children.

Status and Recognition

If this pay graduation strikes you as unreasonable, consider that the potential for failure is much more prevalent in a classroom of high-risk children than it is in a classroom of high-IQ children. The teacher who eliminates the potential failure in a classroom of high-risk children has performed a service that requires a high degree of skill and much patience. This teacher is clearly worth more to the community. Potentially, she has made an enormous difference for most of the children in the class, whereas the teacher of high-IQ children makes a unique contribution for only a few. The teacher of average children is in the middle. Her professional contribution makes a great difference for some of the children, but most could have performed adequately from teachers who have less skill.

In addition to the difference in base salary for teachers of the different classifications of children, the pay scale would call for performance incentives. Their bonus would be determined by the extent to which they exceeded quota. This convention is introduced to induce teachers to do the best job they can and not to reach quota and then stop. It would allow teachers of the average children to make as much as or more than teachers of the high-risk children. Although the formula for computing the bonus is complicated, it would boil down to this: For every twenty percent above quota, the teacher would receive one fifth of her base salary as bonus. The formula would be based on the "median" performance of each instructional group, to make sure that the teacher is not simply accelerating the performance of a few so that she can get a bonus.

There would be no tenure in the system. There would be only yearly contracts for teachers who had worked successfully in the system for one year. If a teacher of average children did not meet quota during the preceding year, she would be demoted to teaching high-IQ children. Similarly, teachers of high-risk children would be demoted one step if they failed to perform. They would have to stay with the average kids for the remainder of the year; then, if they choose to do so, they could return to teaching high-risk children on a four-months'-probation basis.

In most professions the expert practitioner earns at least twice as much as the average practitioner. While the performance pay scale outlined above wouldn't double the salary of the top-performing teachers, it would quickly establish the fact that those who exceed quota with high-risk children are recognized and valued by the system. They have the highest status. They automatically become the models.

The proposed pay scale for primary-grade teachers would probably induce a number of qualified young men to come into the field. As it is, the primary grades (and teaching) hold little promise for advancement for anybody, but opportunities are particularly bleak for somebody who has dependents. The proposed scale would have an appeal for both men and women who were smart and felt that they could stand up under the competition and pounding of a very difficult job. If they could cut it, they would have a good future.

A Plan for Competent Supervisors

I have talked to a number of teachers about the concept of teacher bonuses or merit pay. Surprisingly, most of the good teachers are opposed to it. They indicate that being good is reward enough, and that if a teacher can't get her rewards from knowing she did a good job, she has no business teaching. I agree with them. The biggest reward for a good teacher is the performance of the children. However, the teachers of high-risk children should hold positions of relatively high status. Only the supervisors would hold positions of higher status.

All supervisors would be recruited from the high-risk teachers. To become a supervisor would mean that you have demonstrated for at least two years that you can exceed quota with children who are difficult to teach. A supervisor's first year would be probationary. During the supervisor's second year, she would be given approximately ten teachers who are *not* problems and no more than two who present problems. The new supervisor's work with the two problem teachers would be monitored periodically during the year by an experienced supervisor.

After performing successfully during the second year, the new supervisor would become a full-fledged supervisor. This doesn't mean that the supervisor would receive no more training. All supervisors would attend a summer supervisors' workshop during which they would work with problem children. The point of this training would be to make sure that the supervisors stay ahead of even their best teachers in teaching skills.

The Administration

The principal would have an important management-monitoring function in the system, working closely with the supervisor. He would have four major instructionally related responsibilities:

1. He would see that his teachers (particularly problem teachers) were following the daily schedule, teaching assigned subjects, and making appropriate use of time;

2. He would monitor teachers to see whether they were carrying out specific assignments given by the supervisor;

3. He would report on problems that teachers were experiencing;

4. He would check on excessive absences and teachers who missed in-service sessions.

Although the principal is an administrator and not an instructionalist, he shares many goals with the supervisor. If there is to be pride and *esprit* in his school, it will come from an awareness that the staff does a good job.

The Child Advocate

A final necessary component in the system would be an advocate staff—one advocate for every hundred teachers. The advocates would not be hired by the system, and would not work for the system. They would be successful teachers hired by the school board. They would report directly to the board and would have complete access to all classrooms and all records. Their job would be one not of supervision but of seeing to it that every child within the system received his right of a quality education. They would follow up reports of nonteaching and poor supervision. Teachers, children, parents, administrators, all could alert the advocate staff to problems of children not receiving adequate professional attention by the schools. The advocates would investigate problems and alert the board to them. The board in turn would order the administration to solve the problem. If the school system did not act on it, the advocates would file suit against the system and seek some sort of legal remedy.

The advocates would not run the school system. Nor would their primary function be one of intimidating the system. They would serve as the eyes and ears of the board. They would make it possible for the board to understand some of the technical and real problems in the schools rather than those perfunctory issues that now consume nearly all of the board's time.

Breaking the Cycle of School Incompetence

I suppose that the foregoing description of the ideal school system seems brutal or costly to those who are familiar with the schools as they currently exist. To them it probably seems inhumane to put teachers on probation, and perhaps to fire them if they fail to perform. I can provide only one rejoinder: By what turn of humanitarian arguments could we look a parent in the eye and say, "Too bad that your kid wasn't in Mrs. Beard's classroom—if he had been, he would not have become a school failure, but probably would have performed two grades higher by the time he completed the third grade"?

Perhaps the ideal school system I have outlined (in a very abbreviated way) cannot be achieved. Perhaps the pressure from the educators, the schools, and educational publishers will be great enough to further dupe the public into believing that the schools are doing an acceptable job in discharging their obligation to educate kids. If this happens, we will create a caste system in which smart kids will come from homes in which the kids are taught the kind of skills that are supposed to be taught in the schools. The homes that are more permissive, or less intensive in providing instruction, will produce a relatively high percentage of school failures. The net result will be a predictable pattern, particularly among poor groups, including most of the ethnic minorities. The bulk of children from the "failure" segment of society will fail and will raise failure children. With each generation, the cycle will repeat itself with greater crystallization. And the schools will increasingly throw up their hands and say in effect, "What can we do with all of these kids who aren't ready? Don't blame us for their failure."

To break the cycle, we must put pressure on the schools. If we do it now, we can perhaps avoid a supercrisis. Dealing with the schools, however, is not easy. The schools, like other big bureaucracies, have strong defenses against the kind of change I have proposed. Typically, schools react only to a "loud voice" that threatens the status quo. Since children in school don't have voices and since there are no current provisions for child advocates to speak for these kids, the schools are not obliged to seriously consider the plight of the children. Similarly, the schools don't react to teachers or to people within the community unless they are threatening the status quo. For example, if thirty parents wrote to the administration and told them what a beautiful job Linda had done, there would be no reaction from the administration, because these letters represent no threat to the status quo. One irate letter about Linda wearing a dress that was too short or using foul language in front of the children, however, would bring an immediate reaction from the administration. This letter represents a threat and therefore demands a prompt, and often exaggerated, response which will probably take the form of a hearing.

Despite the defenses of the school system, the system is more vulnerable to attack than the colleges of education or the educational publishers. For the most part, colleges of education are perfectly hopeless. Most people who teach in these institutions have the most limited contact with children or with the realities of the classroom. They will change their training procedures only if they are legislated to do so. The typical response at the college level is to play word games. New words such as "criterion-referenced testing," "relevance," and even "operant conditioning" are absorbed into their vocabularies and integrated with other words, and the change ends at this point. The old procedures persist, buttressed with some new words.

Educational publishers are not easy to change. They are in the business for profit, and will change procedures only if it is more profitable for them to take responsibility for designing instructional programs that work. The demand from the schools for these programs must precede any consistent change in publishing procedures.

The Domino Effect

By forcing the schools to change, we can achieve change in colleges of education and in publishing. Here's how it could happen:

When the public becomes more convinced that the schools are capable of providing real instruction, parents and concerned community groups will begin to harass school districts (with hearings before the board and with lawsuits) for failing to instruct specific children or groups. These plaintiffs will have data showing that similar kids with similar learning problems have been taught successfully. Through suits, the schools will be forced to make a statement about whether they are in the business of teaching kids or merely of watching some kids fail.

The issues in these lawsuits will force the schools to look at their instructional programs, their teaching, and their supervision. As they become cautious, they will start monitoring the classroom scene to make sure that they are not spawning potential lawsuits.

The moment the schools find themselves in the position of dealing with questions of instruction, they will begin to make demands on colleges of education, publishers, and the state boards of higher education. They will say to the colleges, in effect, "Don't send me any more philosophers. We need the kind of teachers who can teach kids and protect us from lawsuits." They will say to the publishers, "Promise less, but *deliver.* Test your programs before you give them to us. Make sure that they admit the instructional game." They will say to the state board of higher education, "Change the certification requirements for teachers. Give us qualified teachers who can protect us from lawsuits." To the departments of public instruction they will say,

"Help us channel federal monies so that we can have a consistent program with adequate personnel."

The school districts will then begin to fight teachers' unions and other groups that front for the organized incompetence of the schools. The schools will find it necessary to issue contracts to teachers that specify the teachers' responsibility for performance of the children and for participating in structured teacher training programs. The teachers' unions may have serious reservations, and some of these will be perfectly justified. Before seventh-grade teachers can perform adequately, the school must first provide them with children who have basic skills and the knowledge that allows them to meet the performance objectives of the seventh grade. There is no way that a teacher can teach children four years of a particular subject in one year. The teachers' groups must protect the teacher against unreasonable demands. The expected outcomes for some children could remain unspecified until the district had some basis for predicting how much growth could be attained with these children during a year of intensive, effective instruction.

In any case, the schools will find themselves in a position of telling teachers' unions and other lobby groups that one issue is not negotiable: the teachers must teach so that children learn. (It may happen that some of the national and local teachers' unions become defendants in lawsuits that relate to incompetence. And it may be that the school district will bring some of these suits against the unions if the unions fail to yield on this nonnegotiable issue.)

The colleges of education will find themselves under attack heavy enough to bring about needed changes in the preparation of teachers. There are a number of intriguing programs that colleges could undertake. One would be to provide students with one year of intensive training (such as Linda participated in), then send the students into the schools to work as aides for two years, then back to the university for a year of more advanced classroom and practicum work that can't be handled efficiently in the schools. Another program might involve high-school students in their junior and senior years who work in a practicum several hours a day. During the next two years, they work in the schools as aides. They would go to the college for one year of advanced classroom and practicum work (perhaps supervising other high-school students). And upon confirmation that they have the various skills needed to present, correct, diagnose, and provide adequate remedies, they would receive a degree and would become certified teachers. Another alternative is to move the colleges of education into the schools, so that the college professors would be involved in the in-service training and the supervision of teachers and aides. All teachers could receive college or advanced credit for mastering specific skills and carrying out quarterly and yearly assignments.

The colleges would quickly recognize that they need people who can deal with the specifics of instruction.

Lawsuits would force the state boards of higher education to scrap their current format for teacher training and introduce new requirements for the training of teachers-to-be, and certification tests to measure whether a teacher has the necessary skills. Currently, most higher boards are guilty of the worst kind of buck-passing. They have dictated the curricula that colleges of education should follow. When reports about the failure in the schools reach them, they turn around and punish the colleges that have followed the specified program to the letter, by reducing funds, closing the colleges, and generally blaming the colleges of education for their failure, when the colleges' real error was in following the decisions of the higher boards.

The response of the school district to suits for malpractice may result in "pure food" laws for publishers of reading programs. The publisher should be responsible for issuing some statement with these programs to indicate that they will produce varying incidence of failure with lower-performing groups of children. The publisher should be required to submit any program considered for publication to a "standardized" field test *with specified kids and a specified format*. Each program would receive a rating. These ratings would reduce the possibility of school districts adopting programs that are totally unreasonable for kids.

Steps for Parents to Take

For this domino effect of change to take place, action must begin with the public at the level of the local schools. This action will terminate either in a lawsuit or in a hearing with the local district. For parents of kids in trouble, take these steps to challenge the schools: (1) a talk with the teacher, (2) classroom observations that document the case, (3) a meeting with the principal for further documentation, (4) an appeal to the board, and (5), possibly, legal action against the school district (or state).

1. A TALK WITH THE TEACHER

Don't wait until your child reaches the fourth grade to spot problems. Try to identify them in the first grade. Here are some of the danger signals to watch for:

> The child consistently brings home worksheets with many of the items marked "Wrong" and not too many marked "Correct."
>
> The child suddenly begins to hate school and goes through rather elaborate routines to avoid going to school.
>
> The child indicates that his reading group is not engaged in reading, although some of the other groups are reading.
>
> The child cannot demonstrate any ability to read by January and you have seen no worksheets or other material that would imply that he can read.
>
> The child expresses a strong dislike for a particular subject, like arithmetic.

Don't interpret a first-grader's vagueness as a sign of trouble. Typically, first-graders are very vague about school and don't respond satisfactorily to questions about the details of what happens in school.

If you notice any of the signs listed above, schedule a meeting with the teacher. There may be no problem, but it's worth an hour of your time to find out.

Find Out What the Problem Is

The traditional attitude of teacher–parent meetings is that the child is on trial and the teacher is the judge who renders the verdict to the parent. Obviously, you will reject this attitude in favor of one in which the school and the teacher are on trial and they are professionally accountable to you. But even though you have this attitude, don't go into the meeting with a chip on your shoulder. Simply try to find out *what the problem is, what the teacher is doing to correct it*, and *what reasons the teacher has for supposing that the solution will work*. Remember, a good teacher usually won't mind answering these questions, unless you labor over them endlessly. Teachers deal with a lot of parents who make unreasonable demands about their children. A teacher's day is long and it requires a great deal of patience. Don't expect the teacher to have an endless supply.

Finding out what the problem is may not be easy. Traditional teachers often describe problems in euphemistic ways, such as "Your child is simply passing through a stage," "He's having some minor adjustment problems right now," or "He's an individual and when he makes up his mind I'm sure he'll have no trouble with school work."

If the teacher casually throws out one of these phrases, recognize that your child is probably in serious trouble. In response to stock phrases such as "He's not quite ready to read, but I'm sure he will be before long," find out specifically what the child cannot do that others in the classroom can do. Have the teacher clarify how his adjustment problem manifests itself or what behavior he exhibits that lets one know that he's not ready or is passing through a stage. Don't be afraid to tell the teacher, "I don't know what it means to say that he is not ready." Require her to elaborate, and insist that the elaboration refer to *behavior*—what the child does and what he is apparently unable to do.

Beware of the judgment "He's working up to his capacity." Ask what the teacher expects the child to be able to do at the end of the year. Find out what "working up to his capacity" actually means. If the teacher continues to be vague about the outcome at the end of the year, ask her if she believes that some of the children may not learn to read during the year, and if so whether it's possible that your child is among them.

In some cases, teachers feel obliged to justify their inability to teach the child by telling you that the child is at fault. Usually, blaming the child takes the form of such statements as "He's extremely hyperactive," "He's immature," "He seems to have a perceptual problem," "He's not ready for instruction," "He has a short attention span." Make the teacher be as specific as possible: "Precisely what does he do that children who are not hyperactive do? How does this behavior affect his reading?" Recognize the possibility that the reason your child is not in the top reading group may be simply that he doesn't belong in that group. Even though the teacher uses expressions such as "immature," she may be providing instruction that is perfectly reasonable. On the other hand, there is no reason why you shouldn't find out what the problem actually is.

The teacher may describe the problem by using quasi-medical terms like "dyslexia," "minimal brain dysfunction," "perceptual handicap," "specific learning disability," or "slow learner." These terms purport to make a statement about the child's capacity to learn. There is no instrument and no informal way to predict what children can learn. The tests for perceptual impairment are simply an inventory of skills. Either children have mastered the specific skills or they haven't. The test implies very little about the child's potential for academic success. The label of "dyslexia" has been rejected by at least two national committees that have studied dyslexia phenomena. Their conclusion was that the use of the term has no possible benefit or application in the educational scene. The word does not imply what one should do to teach children to read.

Find Out Their Proposed Solution

After you have discovered what the problem is, find out what the teacher or the school plans to do about solving the problem. The remedies that the teacher may suggest fall into three categories: remedies that deal directly with the problem behavior, remedies that deal with the *label* that has been assigned to the behavior, and remedies that assume forces beyond the teacher's control.

Here's an example of the first kind of remedy: The child is having trouble learning to read. The teacher is working on each of the skills involved in decoding words. She specifies the skills; she may also indicate what you, the parent, can do to reinforce what she is teaching in school. This remedy is the most straightforward and will probably be the most effective. There is one reservation that you should have. The teacher may be using an impossible reading program. Ask her, "How many children in your classrooms cannot read by the end of the first grade?" If she says, "A couple," or more, your kid's in trouble. If she says, "Usually none unless a child is absent a great deal or enters school late," things look a lot brighter for your kid. You may also want to ask the teacher directly, "Will my kid read reasonably well by the end of the year?"

If the teacher tells you that she is providing a remedy for the *label* she has given the child rather than for the actual behavior, she will not refer to anything as prosaic as working on reading skills. She may indicate that she is working on readiness, perceptual skills, or neurological integration, or on listening activities. These programs don't work. Labels such as "perceptual handicap" are often a form of license that allows the schools to ignore the academic objectives it has established and to introduce a new set of program objectives. The child with the label of perceptual handicap is often taught skills that are supposed to train this perception. He is not taught skills that other children are taught. Alan Cohen of Yeshiva University wrote: "Essentially, the research shows that perceptual motor training results in changes in the behaviors trained. Unless those behaviors are reading behaviors, the perceptual motor training does not produce better reading achievement." If the teacher indicates that your child is receiving a "special" program that teaches perceptual skills (or tunes up his brain in some way), tell her that you will not allow such programs to be used on your child unless the child also receives reading instruction.

Some school districts have perceptual-motor programs for all kids. These kids learn to walk the balance beam; they learn to crawl on all fours; they play rinky-dink games with a patch over one eye; they copy patterns and work on puzzles. And they usually fail in reading as frequently as children in the traditional classroom.

Be suspicious of any program, whether it is in the special class or the regular classroom, that does not directly work on the skills in which the child is weak. If he is placed in a special class, tell the teacher that you would like to see records that show the degree of success the school has in providing "special" children with the skills that other children have. Tell the teacher that if the terminal objectives of this program are not the same as that of the regular program (if the program is not designed to teach the same skills), you will not allow your child to enter the program. Also, find out what measures or tests have been used to determine the need for the special program. There is a good possibility that you would be entitled to a formal hearing if the district wishes to place your child in a special program, particularly if the district uses intelligence tests, such as the Stanford-Binet or the Wechsler. The reason is that these tests are very suspicious in providing meaningful "norms." Both tests were initially tried out on a population consisting of 100 percent white children. In the 1960 revision of the Stanford-Binet, children were excluded from the sample unless the father was living at home. The use of these tests has been successfully challenged in California and in several other states. The basis for the challenge is that the children are stigmatized by a test that has not been demonstrated to be a valid instrument at predicting school achievement or the child's "intelligence."

The teacher using a remedy based on forces beyond the school's control will be vague about what she is doing to correct the problem. She may suggest that she is giving the child time to adjust, or that she is holding off reading instruction to keep from "pressuring" him. She may indicate that in time he will become *motivated* to read and that she will simply wait for him to become motivated or ready.

Placing the Teacher on Notice

Let the teacher know that you reject any remedy that involves time for maturation, time for readiness to develop, or time for the child to adjust, on the grounds that the school is discriminating against your child. Explain to the teacher that she must teach the child the skills in which he is weak. If she suggests that he won't be able to keep up with the class, explain that giving him the same lessons as the other members of the class is not the solution to strengthening his skills. Tell her that you are not interested in *how* the teacher manages to give the child needed skills; you are interested in the child's performance. Ask her if she feels capable of teaching him. If not, then the child should be placed with a teacher who has more confidence in her professional ability. If the teacher indicates that she could teach the child effectively if it weren't for class size or schedules, she is actually telling you that she is not capable of teaching him. (She may be giving you very reasonable reasons for her inability.) However, if she is incapable of providing instruction, the capacity of the school becomes suspect. Your child should not suffer disproportionately because of the school's inadequacies.

Take notes during the meeting and, before you leave, read aloud to the teacher and ask her if you have misrepresented what she said about any issue. Make any necessary corrections or additions.

You may leave the meeting with a feeling that the teacher will provide adequate instruction for your kid. It is possible, however, that you will leave with the impression that the teacher is incapable or unwilling to attack the instructional problems.

2. CLASSROOM OBSERVATIONS

Assuming that the teacher does not satisfy you about the kind of instruction she is giving your child, call the principal and tell him that you wish to observe the classroom during the period that the problem subject is being taught. Take a tape recorder with you if you have access to one. It's a good idea to get permission to observe on more than one day. When you observe, don't talk to your child. Don't walk around the room and look at what other kids are doing. Don't do anything that would create a "distraction." Sit, take notes, and turn on your tape recorder.

Document (1) every case of extreme management problem; (2) any tasks or activities that the children don't seem to understand after the teacher has completed her teaching and has moved to another activity; and (3) any tasks or activities presented during the reading period that don't seem to have a direct bearing on the subject being taught. Note whether the teacher works with small groups or presents to the entire class.

Before you leave, ask the teacher about each activity that flopped or didn't seem to relate to the subject the teacher was supposed to teach. You may observe that the teacher presents "listening activities" to the "slow" group during the reading period. Ask the teacher the purpose of this activity. She will probably tell you that it teaches the children how to listen, and that it will build up their listening skills. Ask her what kind of listening skills are required to begin reading and which of those your child doesn't have. Ask her about any tasks or activities that seemed too difficult for the children, particularly for the children who have trouble with the subject. Ask her if the activity is necessary. (Often the teacher knows that certain specific skills are important, yet has no "plan" for making sure that the children master these skills.) Don't argue with her; write down or record her response.

Make sure that when you leave you have the teacher's rationale for every type of general activity that seems to have no relationship to the problem subject.

3. A Meeting with the Principal

The third step after the classroom observation is to schedule a meeting with the principal. Tell the principal that you want to talk to *him*—not to him and the teacher. Explain that you want to ask him some questions about the instruction that your child is receiving in school. Your goal is to document that he doesn't know very much about the instruction your child is receiving. The odds are about ten to one that at this point you have far more information about the teacher and the instruction she provides than the principal has. Expect the principal to be somewhat defensive. Many traditional principals will swear that their teachers are the best in the world, but upon further investigation one often discovers that the principal doesn't know what goes on in the classroom.

Again take your tape recorder with you. Begin by asking the principal what he thinks of your child's teacher. "Do you think she's a competent professional?" In the improbable event that the principal says "No," the next question would be "Why, then, are you letting her teach twenty-seven children?" If the answer is "Yes," ask him the basis for his conclusion. He will probably speak in vague terms about her dedication, energy, personality, and concern. After he has completed his tribute, ask if you can see the data on the performance of children who were in her classroom last year. If she is a new teacher, ask if he has any basis for judging her effectiveness as a teacher.

The principal may be reluctant to show you records of the teacher's performance for the preceding year, saying, "Our files are confidential." Then ask, "Did any children fail to learn to read by the end of the year? . . . How many children were substantially below grade level at the end of the year? . . . How many children do you expect will be either failures or substantially below grade level at the end of this year?" If he doesn't know, then indicate that you will call him after he has a chance to check his "confidential" records.

Next, find out *his* rationale for the questionable activities you have observed in the classroom. Describe any activities that either seemed inappropriate or were apparently too difficult for the children. Ask him what the school's justification is for presenting that activity or for using that procedure. The principal will probably indicate that the teacher should be present to answer these questions. Explain to him that you have already asked the teacher, but you want to understand the school's position. If the principal says that the teacher makes the judgment about such activities, indicate that you find it difficult to believe that the teachers are not accountable to anybody. "Who can speak for the school and explain why the teacher uses that activity?"

Ask the principal what kind of monitoring the teacher receives to find out whether she is doing an acceptable job. Ask whether the school selected the instructional material the teacher is using.

After you have interviewed the principal, tell him that you are not satisfied with the instruction your child is receiving and that the teacher must begin to teach the child satisfactorily or the child must be assigned to another teacher. Indicate further that you are not interested in whether the child will receive some sort of social promotion at the end of the year; you expect him to have mastered the skills that he will be required to use in the next grade. (If you discover that your child has received a social promotion, establish that the principal and the teacher understand that the child doesn't have the skills needed to perform in the next grade, yet they passed him.)

The last important thing you wish to document is that there is not one person in the entire administration whose job it is to identify the problems the teacher has or to show the teacher specifically how to solve specific teaching problems. If you have observed classroom activities in which not all of the children performed adequately (or in which the teacher received feedback from only those few children who raised their hands), pass your observation along to the principal and then ask, "What provisions are there for making the teacher more effective? Specifically, who shows her how to teach the various tasks she presents, and what provisions are there for training?"

The principal will probably indicate that there are curriculum or elementary supervisors who regularly "visit" the classroom. Ask the principal whether these supervisors can teach the exercises with which the teacher is having trouble. Also find out the frequency of the supervisor's visits, the content covered, and the nature of follow-up on specific assignments. Find out which demonstrations have been provided to the teacher over the year.

The principal will probably be unable to answer any of these questions, because there is only one chance in a hundred that there is a supervisor in the district who can teach the various exercises so that the children master the skills, or who has clear responsibility for working with teachers on specific curricular problems. The reason is that these supervisors have been appointed on the basis of their political skills, not their teaching skills. In many school districts, the job specifications for supervisors indicate that they are to work with teachers, but the description of activities is often vague. The job specifications may provide ammunition for your attack, however.

4. APPEAL TO THE BOARD

The next step is to present your case to the school board (unless you live in a community such as Providence, Rhode Island, which has a "Department of Education"). Call the board and indicate that you would like time at a board meeting to present the problem. If the board does not see fit to put you on the agenda, write a detailed letter to the editor of your newspaper in which you describe the problem in the most factual, unemotional manner you can manage. Document three points in the letter: (1) the teacher is not dealing directly with the problem; (2) the principal is not actually aware of what goes on in the classroom; and (3) the various supervisors have provided no help to the teacher in becoming more effective.

If the board permits you to present at a meeting, document the points above. Make the point that there seem to be no uniform provisions in the school system for protecting children against failure. Find out from the board what it plans to do about the problem.

It is difficult to predict how the board will react to a well-documented case (one that is obviously prepared with litigation in mind). Often board members have far more common sense than professional educators. They will probably appreciate the problem but are likely to be frustrated after conferring with the administration in an attempt to solve it. They may discover that the administration is not aware of the failure rate produced by different teachers. The board will probably try to offer some kind of solution. This may involve moving the kid to another classroom or perhaps allowing you to take the child out of school, possibly with the school paying for the outside instruction. (There have been lawsuits dealing with the school's responsibility for paying tuition for children who are not placed appropriately in school programs. The outcome of these suits has not been generally encouraging.)

5. LEGAL ACTION

The final step would be a lawsuit against the district or the state. From a political standpoint, it is a good idea to initiate strong lawsuits even if the odds are substantially against a favorable decision. The publicity and the harassment value of the suits may force school administrators to review their quality-control procedures to see what they can do to improve the school's image.

On the other hand, lawsuits are expensive. And the preparation of a suit against the school would be extensive, particularly because lawyers are unfamiliar with this type of action and because the courts experience an understandable degree of concern about the social consequences of establishing new legal precedents.

To reduce the cost, you might join with other parents who are in a similar situation and split the cost. If your child is in the slow group, contact parents of the other kids in that group and see if any are willing to participate. It may be that local or state legal services would be available, particularly if the case dealt with civil rights of the children. Contact the American Civil Liberties Union or similar agencies to see if they would be able to arrange legal counsel.

Steps for Teachers

Recognize that you will probably be held accountable for the performance of children in your classroom within the next five to ten years. If you wish to stay in teaching, begin to protect yourself against possible malpractice suits. Here are a few things you can do:

1. Demand help with specific exercises that are not working with your children. Put your request in writing to your supervisor. Make it quite clear that you have tried to follow the program or the syllabus and that the children are not responding adequately. Request immediate assistance in the way of a demonstration and training in how to present the material in a way that will teach the children. Send a request for every important exercise that gives you trouble. Keep a record of all requests.

2. Use a similar procedure if you are saddled with an impossible schedule. If you are to cover an entire year of arithmetic

with a time allocation of seventy minutes a week, demand a demonstration from your supervisor of how one handles the program successfully in the allotted time.

3. Send written statements of protest about every child placed in your grade who is severely lacking in skills needed to handle the material that you are assigned to cover during the year. Point out the time problems confronting you if you are to teach these children at a level suited to their ability and also teach the other children according to the syllabus. Be specific and detailed.

4. Demand on-the-job training for any new instructional program that is installed. If you are to be held accountable for the children's performance in this program, you deserve the kind of training that concentrates on the key teaching behaviors and that has been demonstrated to work. Don't run the risk of doing the program the wrong way. Make sure that you thoroughly understand what you are supposed to do and what you are not supposed to do. Insist on guided practice sessions, with detailed feedback.

5. Point out (in writing) to administrators if the training provided on a particular program is not effective. The test is relatively simple: If the training allowed you to succeed and teach all of your children successfully, the training worked. If you have problems, the training apparently didn't work.

The steps above not only protect you from possible malpractice suits; they also provide the administration with the kinds of details it must have to know if the programs it has installed are going smoothly. If there are problems, the administration must know which teachers have the problems and which exercises seem to be the most troublesome. The administrators must know whether teachers have adequate supervision. If a few dozen complaints come to one supervisor every day (which is what should happen if teachers followed the procedures outlined above), the administrators would quickly realize that much more supervision is needed. If the administrators learned that the supervisors were not capable of answering the teachers' questions and of providing effective demonstrations of how to present specific exercises, they would realize that their supervisors are not up to the job. This information would perhaps prompt administrators to look for teachers who have demonstrated the kind of teaching success a supervisor must have.

Another thing you should do is use your union to support the professional aspects of teaching. A union is designed to protect teachers. Its goal is to see that they have a reasonable life and receive reasonable recompense for their efforts in the classroom. These goals are admirable if they are kept in the realistic perspective that schools are designed for kids, not teachers. Teachers are placed in schools because they have a professional responsibility for the kids. The union should be as protective of this professional responsibility as it is of the creature comforts of teachers. If unions are to help teachers achieve and maintain a professional status, they must (1) take a firm stand on the issue that the performance of the children is the only indicator that tells whether teaching has taken place, (2) help establish suitable procedures for firing or changing the behavior of incompetent teachers, (3) demand the kind of in-service training and supervision that are needed if programs are to succeed, and (4) support effective programs (rather than those that are the most palatable to teachers).

Steps for Administrators

What can administrators do to protect themselves against malpractice suits?

1. If you have scrapped an instructional program because it didn't work and if you have evidence about why it didn't work, send the information to the publisher of the program and to the local colleges of education. These people are far removed from the classroom. They need this information.

2. If you are thinking of scrapping a program because it doesn't work, call in the publisher. Show him what you've done

to train the teachers. Ask him what you should do to make the program work. Follow his suggestions, if they seem manageable. Send him a report on the success of his recommendations.

3. Don't accept certified teachers without giving them a test—a half-day demonstration with children of the age they are to work with. The current ratio of teachers to available jobs is ten to one, even more in many communities. You don't have to hire incompetents from a university or from another school district. If you have five jobs, bring in twenty-five candidates and let them show you what they've got. Make sure that a competent supervisor observes, questions them, and evaluates their teaching ability.

4. Every time you reject a certified teacher on the basis that she doesn't have the technical equipment necessary for the job, write to the university from which she came and also write the state certification board. They need this information.

5. Provide for evaluation of every new teacher by a supervisor. Send a copy of this evaluation to the university from which she graduated and to the state certification board.

6. Try to implement criterion-referenced testing, carefully sequenced instructional programs, adequate in-service training, and adequate supervision. When you are blocked, put it in writing. If the board doesn't provide financial backing, explain in writing your position and the possible consequences of the board's action. Your best protection against a malpractice suit is a detailed documentation of your efforts to implement a system that will work.

Steps for Parents, Teachers, and Administrators

Beware of educational philosophies that are basically discriminatory. Many are, although they are often presented by liberals who seem to care and who are concerned about the "establishment." They often call others racists (sometimes with good reason). Here are some quick guides to spotting a racist or at best one who discriminates against some kids:

1. A person who advocates different educational standards for different ethnic groups, with lower standards assigned to particular groups, is a purveyor of a racist argument. If we don't teach blacks to read, or teach them other academic skills than are typically taught to white middle-class children, we are establishing a *prima facie* basis for discriminating against blacks. They won't be able to go to college, because they won't have the skills. They will not have the range of choices that other children have. A demographer can then complete the cycle by pointing out that our best educational efforts have "failed" with these children and that their scores on a range of instruments indicate racial inferiority.

A double standard in terminal objectives can lead only to discrimination. The college that awards degrees to ethnic students who lack skill is operating from a double standard. We must provide instruction that honors a child's starting point. The end product must be the same in terms of competence.

2. A person who advocates programs or formats that clearly favor children with skills not taught in the school is advocating discrimination. The most extreme example is the person who advocates closing the public schools. Who would benefit disproportionately if the schools were closed? The very wealthy would send their children to private schools (as many already do). The middle-class child would be in the middle. He would probably learn a great deal of school-related skills at home, and perhaps he would also go to a private school. The poor child from the ghetto, however, would not have this option. He would have to learn skills from the neighborhood, where academic skills are not frequently bandied about. The kid who needs education would suffer enormously from the closing of the kind of school that actually met his educational needs.

3. Another form of discriminatory argument holds that the child should be given the choice of what he is to learn. The format may be the open classroom or miscellaneous unsupervised activities that are supposed to lead to the child's "discovery" of important knowledge. Children have the right to be children. As

children, they don't know enough to make choices that will affect their lives in important ways. To allow the child to make decisions now that will seriously affect his success later in school is to treat the child like an adult, not a child. Such permission will discriminate against those children who choose to make decisions that limit their future choices and decrease the possibility of a "harmonious" school adjustment.

4. A person who argues that different ethnic groups have no deficiencies is purveying not only an untruth but a discriminatory one. Although it is fashionable to say that the average ghetto black does not have academic problems, the statement runs counter to every observation that one makes in the classroom. This is not to say that *all* ghetto black children have trouble or that even those who exhibit problems are "inferior." The assumption is that they are basically intelligent and that they are capable of the same academic achievement that the more affluent child obtains. It is difficult to solve a problem if we aren't honest about the nature of that problem, however. If we don't face the typical academic problems of the ghetto black, we probably won't solve them. To fail to solve them is to discriminate against him. He was placed in situations that assumed skills he didn't have. Clearly, the school system is guilty of malpractice—if not legally, at least morally. And the parents have every right to hold the school accountable if it promotes the child rather than work on the deficient skills.

We have compromised in the schools, and through our compromises the primary role of the school has lost focus. Educators have arrogated to themselves the role of establishing *goals* of education—a role that is not theirs, has never been theirs, and hopefully will never be theirs. The educators have successfully made platforms of such issues as the new learning center, the athletic program, and the busing plan. At the same time, they have managed to obscure the more fundamental issues of instruction.

Traditional education proclaims that the school is society in microcosm. Actually, the school bears little resemblance to society at large. There is one issue, however, that seems to be a microcosmic projection of a larger societal issue. That is: To what extent are we willing to compromise? In society, there is reluctance to stand up to any loud demands, regardless of how preposterous they are. The same tendency pervades the schools. Any loud demands from teachers, administrators, or renowned educators seem to become a credible demand, and we yield.

By yielding, we compromise two rights of the children—the moral (if not legal) right to receive an education, and the right to be a child, not an adult in miniature. A child has the right to the care and protection his family provides. If an agency assumes functions of the parents through mandated education, the care and protection must remain. We don't allow children to negotiate in the doctor's office or in the presence of some immediate danger. Why should we treat education as any more negotiable than good health?

Let's declare a moratorium on statements about democracy in the school (where policy is dictated by a few). Let's abolish double standards for children with different ethnic backgrounds. Let's acknowledge that we may have to work harder with some kids to bring them to a high level of competence, but that we have a strong commitment to bring all kids at least to a reasonable level of competency.

Above all, let's recognize that a real teacher can come as close to performing miracles as anybody. It is difficult to place a price tag on the services that she provides for the community. She opens doors for potential failures; she instills hope; she changes their lives in a way that no doctor, social worker, or other community agent can.

Let's do more than give lip service to the rights of children. Let's translate our understanding of their rights into procedures that protect them from incompetence, indifference, and malpractice.

Notes and Bibliography

Chapter 1

The staffing procedures dramatized in this chapter are firmly established by tradition, particularly in schools serving affluent areas. For a more formal description of standard staffing procedures, see R. J. Margolin and A. C. Williamson's *Case Conferences in Education* (Boston: Bruce Humphries, 1961), or other basic counseling and guidance texts. A more direct approach would be to talk with the school psychologist in your nearest affluent district.

Chapter 3

The labels given children and the categories into which they are placed are presented in any introductory special-education text. For example, descriptions of the mentally retarded, visually or orthopedically handicapped, speech- or hearing-impaired, gifted, emotionally disturbed, and learning-disabled may be found in S. A. Kirk's *Educating Exceptional Children* (Boston:

Houghton Mifflin, 1962), or L. M. Dunn's (ed.) *Exceptional Children in the Schools* (New York: Holt, Rinehart & Winston, 1963).

Recently, labeling of "mentally handicapped" has come under legal scrutiny. Better articles on the subject include F. Wientraub and A. Abeson, "Appropriate Education for All Handicapped Children: A Growing Issue," *Syracuse Law Review,* 1972, No. 23, pp. 1037–58, and a very comprehensive commentary, "Segregation of Poor and Minority Children into Classes for the Mentally Retarded by Use of IQ Tests," *Michigan Law Review,* 1973, No. 71, pp. 1212–50.

Papers by Barbara D. Bateman ("Educational Implications of Minimal Brain Dysfunction") and S. Alan Cohen ("Minimal Brain Dysfunction and Practical Matters Such as Teaching Kids to Read"), both presented before the New York Academy of Sciences' Conference on Minimal Brain Dysfunction, New York, 1972, argue against the use of labels quite convincingly.

The "talking typewriter" of Omar Khayyam Moore, which was widely adopted before careful verification of its effectiveness, is discussed by Moore and A. R. Anderson in R. D. Hess and R. M. Bear's (eds.) *Early Education: Current Theory, Research, and Action* (Chicago: Aldine, 1966). An earlier article may be found in J. Hellmuth's (ed.) *The Special Child in Century 21* (Seattle: Special Child Publications, 1963).

Glenn Nimnict has written about another version of the "talking typewriter" in an article called "Low-cost Typewriter Approach Helps Preschoolers Type Words and Stories," *Nation's Schools,* 1967, No. 80, pp. 34–37. There is no compelling data to suggest that the typewriter is a viable instructional tool, although it may be a good reinforcing tool.

The supposed effects of teachers expecting children who are falsely labeled as latent learners to blossom were presented by

Robert Rosenthal and Lenore Jacobson in *Pygmalion in the Classroom* (New York: Holt, Rinehart & Winston, 1968). Attempts to experimentally reproduce the results that Rosenthal and Jacobson obtained have failed. For reports of these later studies see W. L. Clairborn's "Expectancy Effects in the Classroom: A Failure to Replicate," *Journal of Educational Psychology,* 1969, No. 60, pp. 377–83, or N. J. Jose's "Teacher Expectancies and Classroom Interaction," a paper presented before the American Educational Research Association meeting in Minneapolis, 1970.

An analysis by W. C. Becker of the performance of teachers and children in the Engelmann-Becker Follow Through project is summarized in "Some Necessary Conditions for the Controlled Study of Achievement and Aptitude" in D. R. Green (ed.), *The Aptitude–Achievement Distinction* (Monterey, Calif.: C.T.B./McGraw-Hill, 1974).

Becker's analysis discloses that a child's IQ in kindergarten does not correlate significantly with his third-grade performance. Even the child's achievement the previous year does not accurately predict his current performance. The *only* variable which correlates significantly with the children's achievement is the *specific teaching behaviors of the teacher* (such as amount of time devoted to instruction and specific techniques used to correct mistakes, etc.).

The two studies by Walker and his associates which are referred to in the text are: H. M. Walker and N. K. Buckley, "Teacher Attention to Appropriate and Inappropriate Classroom Behavior: An Individual Case Study," *Focus on Exceptional Children,* 1973, No. 5, pp. 5–11; and H. M. Walker, W. E. Fiegenbaum, and H. Hops, *Components Analysis and Systematic Replication of a Treatment Model for Modifying Deviant Classroom Behavior,* Report No. 3, Center at Oregon for Research in the Behavioral Education of the Handicapped (Eugene, Ore.: University of Oregon, 1971).

Chapter 4

Of the numerous books, articles, and speeches by B. F. Skinner, perhaps the presentation with the most direct value for teaching is *The Technology of Teaching* (New York: Appleton-Century-Crofts, 1968).

Don Bushell, Jr., has written a clear and thorough introduction to the uses of operant conditioning techniques in classrooms, called *Classroom Behavior: A Little Book for Teachers* (Englewood Cliffs, N.J.: Prentice-Hall, 1973).

Information about the learning center at Fort Meade, Md., is contained in "Report on the Anne Arundel Learning Center," by Shlomo I. Cohen (unpublished paper, Anne Arundel County Board of Education, Annapolis, Maryland, November 1969).

Some studies by Wes Becker and associates that illustrate the use of operant techniques include "An Analysis of the Reinforcing Function of 'Sit Down' Commands," by C. H. Madsen, W. C. Becker, D. R. Thomas, L. Koser, and E. Plager, in R. K. Parker (ed.), *Readings in Educational Psychology* (Boston: Allyn and Bacon, 1968); "The Contingent Use of Teacher Attention and Praise in Reducing Classroom Behavior Problems," by W. C. Becker, C. H. Madsen, C. R. Arnold, and D. R. Thomas, in *Journal of Special Education*, 1967, No. 1, pp. 287–307; "Production and Elimination of Disruptive Classroom Behaviors by Systematically Varying Teacher's Behavior," by D. R. Thomas, W. C. Becker, and M. Armstrong, in *Journal of Applied Behavior Analysis*, 1968, No. 1, pp. 35–45; and "Rules, Praise, and Ignoring: Elements of Elementary Classroom Control," by C. H. Madsen, W. C. Becker, and D. R. Thomas, in *Journal of Applied Behavior Analysis*, 1968, No. 1, pp. 139–50.

The Journal of Applied Behavior Analysis consistently provides information about some of the most practical uses of operant techniques. It is published quarterly by the Society of the Experimental Analysis of Behavior, Inc., Department of Human Development, University of Kansas, Lawrence, Kans.

The study on gratifying children's needs referred to in the text is reported in F. L. Strodtbeck, "Progress Report: The Reading Readiness Nursery: Short-term Intervention Technique" (a mimeo paper, University of Chicago Social Psychology Lab, 1964).

Crisis in the Classroom, edited by Charles Silberman, is published by Random House (New York, 1970).

It is interesting to note that the model school referred to in the text has abandoned the open-classroom model in favor of periods of more highly structured work. The change has had a salutary effect on the performance of the children.

Chapter 5

To look at the course offerings for teacher education, one might be impressed by the titles and descriptions of the courses. However, the rule seems to be that the descriptions have little bearing on what is actually taught. For example, the 1973–75 general catalogue for Iowa State University lists twenty courses for the Department of Elementary Education. (There are additional courses listed by other departments in the college, including "foundation" courses.) Precisely one of the listed courses refers to the teaching of reading—Course 375. It presents "approaches to developmental teaching of reading in elementary schools; emphasis on techniques, materials, skills, literature, innovations, issues, evaluation, procedures, and reading in the content areas." I would like to meet the instructor who could even *introduce* those topics with less than complete casuistry in one year. Iowa State is on the quarter system.

Not all courses of study are *prima facie* hopeless. The undergraduate catalogue for Eastern Connecticut State College lists over forty education courses for 1972–73. Four of these deal with reading: developmental reading, the teaching of reading, reading in the middle grades, and reading in the primary grades. According to the catalogue, in the first course, developmental reading, "Considerations will be given to the problems and procedures in developing a functional reading program for the elementary grades. It will include word identification skills, study skills, materials of instruction, and grouping. There will be demonstrations and projects." It could be done, and it could be done well as an introduction. The subsequent courses are also feasible, so far as their description goes. It may be that students who take all three courses for elementary teaching of reading courses for a total of nine semester hours and student teaching emerge from Eastern Connecticut with the knowledge of a practitioner. Maybe.

The Aubrey Haan book referred to in the body of this chapter is *Education for the Open Society* (Boston: Allyn and Bacon, 1962).

The Albert Harris text is *Effective Teaching of Reading* (New York: David McKay, 1962).

The Miles Zintz book is *Corrective Reading* (Dubuque, Iowa: William C. Brown, 1972).

A book edited by Barbara D. Bateman, *Reading Performance and How to Achieve It* (Seattle: Bernie Straub Publishing Co., Special Child Publications, 1973), includes several studies which compare different approaches to reading instruction.

An earlier book of my own, *Preventing Failure in the Primary Grades* (Chicago: Science Research Associates, 1969), lays out step-by-step activities for teachers to use in the classroom.

Chapter 6

There are nine DISTAR programs, all published by Science Research Associates, Chicago: *DISTAR Reading* 1, 2, 3; *DISTAR Arithmetic* 1, 2, 3; *DISTAR Language* 1, 2, 3. The rationale for some of the critical aspects of each program is presented in the book *Preventing Failure in the Primary Grades* (Chicago: Science Research Associates, 1969).

Other instructional programs referred to in this chapter include *Harper & Row Basic Reading Program* (New York: Harper & Row, 1966); *Probing into Science* (New York: American Book Co., 1968); *Exploring Elementary Mathematics Patterns and Structure* (New York: Holt, Rinehart & Winston, 1970); *Our Big World* (Morristown, N.J.: Silver Burdett, 1961); and *English 4* (River Forest, Ill.: Laidlaw Brothers, 1967). These are not exceptionally poor programs; pick up just about any text —particularly one written for fourth-grade children—and you will probably be shocked by the assumptions of skill and knowledge made by the authors.

Data on the effectiveness of instructional programs may be found in a variety of sources. Perhaps the best single book on reading programs is by Jeanne Chall, *Learning to Read: The Great Debate* (New York: McGraw-Hill, 1967). Chall concludes that the more structured and phonically oriented programs are most likely to teach reading adequately.

More recently, Barbara D. Bateman's collection of articles, *Reading Performance and How to Achieve It* (Seattle: Bernie Straub Publishing Co., Special Child Publications, 1973), provides similar evidence.

Why Johnny Can't Read and What You Can Do about It (New York: Harper and Brothers, 1955), by Rudolf Flesch, is generally acknowledged as marking a turning point in the area of reading instruction.

The data on the Engelmann-Becker Follow Through model presented in this chapter may be found in "Some Effects of Direct Instruction Methods in Teaching Disadvantaged Children in Project Follow Through," by W. C. Becker, published in *Proceedings of the International Symposium on Behavior Therapy* (New York: Appleton-Century-Crofts, 1973).

Chapter 7

The first conceptualization of the criterion-referenced measure came in Robert Glaser's article "Instructional Technology and the Measurement of Learning Outcomes: Some Questions," *American Psychologist*, 1963, No. 18, pp. 519–21. Those who picked up on it apparently lost sight of the game, which was to assess the effectiveness of instruction, not to impose instruction on the teacher and the student. Most of the "programs" of testing (such as SCORE, ostensibly a custom-designed criterion-referenced service, offered by the Westinghouse Learning Corporation and the Croft Inservice Program) purport to provide criterion-referenced measures. They don't, for the simple reason that you can't have a criterion-referenced measure unless it tests the instructional programs already used in the classroom. Without accepting this seemingly logical requirement, the criterion-referenced test becomes another dumping ground. Any test could be called a criterion-referenced test.

Consider this sample item from the Westinghouse Learning Corporation:

> [Administrator's text] The teacher says: "Read the story to yourselves." (Pause.) "Have you finished?" (You may help them with unfamiliar words.) "Now look at the names below the story. Cover the story with your hand and darken the space under the name of Bob's dog."

The item presented to the children is:

Bob is six years old. He lives in California. He has a dog named Ivan and a cat named Emily. He likes his pets very much.

Emily	Bob	Rover	Ivan
A	B	C	D

From a criterion-referenced standpoint, this item would be allowable only if those inane instructions were part of the children's regular reading program or if items of a similar format were presented in the reading program. But who gave the criterion-referenced test license to impose possibly new teaching on the children, which is what would happen if the children failed the item and the teacher wanted them to pass? She would have to teach skills that are not part of her regular program. Furthermore, the test item is designed so that it cannot possibly yield clear diagnostic information—the kind that is needed in the criterion-referenced-test game. If the child fails the item, you can shake your head and say, "My, my," just as you can with any standardized test. The rule is: You can't have criterion-referenced tests apart from specific instructional programs.

See also W. Otto and E. N. Askov, *The Wisconsin Design for Reading Skill Development, Rationale, and Guidelines* (Minneapolis, Minn.: National Computer Systems, 1970).

If you want to look at a perfectly preposterous "criterion-referenced" system, see the Croft Inservice Program, *Reading Word-Attack Skills, a Systems Approach,* by J. L. Cooper and M. L. McGuire (New London, Conn.: Croft Education Services, 1973).

The achievement tests referred to in this chapter are *The Gates-MacGinitie Reading Test* (New York: Teachers' College, Columbia University, 1965), which comes in a variety of forms and levels (the information cited in this chapter refers principally to the primary forms), and *The Metropolitan Achievement Test* (New York: Harcourt Brace Jovanovich, 1970).

These tests are similar to other standardized achievement tests used by the schools. They are also suspect, particularly in terms of the children used to arrive at designations of "grade level" performance.

Chapter 8

Over the past few years, there has been an increasing concern with the legal aspects of teaching, although most of what is written does not concern itself with professional practices and protection against malpractice. Don Stewart's book *Educational Malpractice, the Big Gamble in Our Schools* (Pasadena, Calif.: Slate Services, 1971) presents a comprehensive outline of the various kinds of malpractices of which the schools are guilty. The legal remedies he suggests are probably not as sophisticated as his grasp of the malpractices. The book is interesting. Read it.

Perhaps the most thorough article on the kinds of remedies that may be possible if your school does not teach healthy children is contained in the article "If Johnny Can't Read—Get Yourself a Lawyer," by Stephen P. Sugarman, in *Learning*, 1974, No. 2, pp. 26–31. Sugarman deals in a direct manner with the problem of *learning*, suggesting possible actions of fraud, malpractice, etc. Most of the other articles on the subject don't deal with the problem of learning. Rather, they deal with whether the child is physically in a place called a school that has officially declared that it has a program appropriate for that kid.

The laws for dealing with the school failure and the handicapped child are very nebulous. Even the question of whether the handicapped child has a right to *be* in school and the terms under which he is to be excluded present many legal questions. If you're interested, these are discussed quite adequately in an article by Suzanne K. Richards and Lois G. Williams, titled "Toward a Legal Theory of the Right to Education of the Mentally Retarded," which appeared in the *Ohio State Law Journal,* 1973, No. 34, pp. 554–85.

For a discussion of the legal issues associated with discrimination on racial and ethnic grounds, read "Segregation of Poor and Minority Children into Classes for the Mentally Retarded by Use of IQ Tests," in the *Michigan Law Review,* 1973, No. 71, pp. 1212–50.

An article by Paul Gordon, "Public Instruction to the Learning Disabled: Higher Hurdles for the Handicapped," *University of San Francisco Law Review,* 1973, No. 8, pp. 113–48, quoted in this chapter, surveys the landmark decisions concerning education for those with learning disabilities, in an attempt to arrive at an articulation of the constitutional and legal rights of such children.

Patrick J. Casey in his article "The Supreme Court and the Suspect Class," *Exceptional Children,* 1973, No. 39, pp. 119–25, cautions administrators, legislators and others not to assume that their obligations to handicapped students have been ended because of recent court decisions. He discusses the ploy described earlier in this chapter of establishing a suspect class and outlines the prerequisites and implications of such an approach.

About the Author

SIEGFRIED ENGELMANN is professor of special education at the University of Oregon, co-director of the Engelmann-Becker Follow Through model (which serves projects in twenty U.S. communities), president of the Engelmann-Becker Corporation (which provides material and training to school districts), research associate at Oregon Research Institute (where he is conducting research on tactual communication with deaf children), father of four, and husband. He is author of many instructional programs, including all of the DISTAR programs. He has written over a dozen books and manuals, including *Give Your Child a Superior Mind* and *Preventing Failure in the Primary Grades.*